IRENAEUS

IRENAEUS

Denis Minns OP

GEORGETOWN UNIVERSITY PRESS

For Bernice
in memory of Jack

Georgetown University Press, Washington, D.C. 20007
Geoffrey Chapman, a Cassell imprint, London, England

© Denis Minns OP 1994

First published 1994

Library of Congress Cataloging-in-Publication Data
Minns, Denis.
   Irenaeus / Denis Minns.
     p.   cm.
   Includes bibliographical references.
   ISBN 0-87840-553-4
   1. Irenaeus, Saint. Bishop of Lyon. 2. Theology, Doctrinal—
History—Early church. ca. 30-600. I. Title.
BR1720.I7M56 1994
230'.14'092—dc20   93-36686
                                           CIP

Typeset by Colset Private Limited, Singapore
Printed and bound in Great Britain by
Biddles Ltd, Guildford and King's Lynn

Contents

Editorial foreword

St Anselm of Canterbury once described himself as someone with faith seeking understanding. In words addressed to God he says 'I long to understand in some degree thy truth, which my heart believes and loves. For I do not seek to understand that I may believe, but I believe in order to understand.'

And this is what Christians have always inevitably said, either explicitly or implicitly. Christianity rests on faith, but it also has content. It teaches and proclaims a distinctive and challenging view of reality. It naturally encourages reflection. It is something to think about; something about which one might even have second thoughts.

But what have the greatest Christian thinkers said? And is it worth saying? Does it engage with modern problems? Does it provide us with a vision to live by? Does it make sense? Can it be preached? Is it believable?

This series originates with questions like these in mind. Written by experts, it aims to provide clear, authoritative and critical accounts of outstanding Christian writers from New Testament times to the present. It will range across the full spectrum of Christian thought to include Catholic and Protestant thinkers, thinkers from East and West, thinkers ancient, mediaeval and modern.

The series draws on the best scholarship currently available, so it will interest all with a professional concern for the history of Christian ideas. But contributors will also be writing for general readers who have little or no previous knowledge of the subjects to be dealt with. Volumes to appear should therefore prove helpful at a popular as well as an academic level. For the most part they will be devoted to a single thinker, but occasionally the subject will be a movement or school of thought.

The *Oxford Dictionary of the Christian Church* (2nd revised edn, 1983) calls the subject of the present volume 'the first great Catholic theologian'. In the pages which follow, Fr Denis Minns explains why this is an accurate description. Much scholarly work has been done on Irenaeus and his period in recent years, and much of it is noted by Fr Minns. His book, however, is principally an introduction to the theology of Irenaeus rather than an introduction to the problems involved in reading him. Readers, I think, will find it comprehensive, informative, lucid and elegantly written. It is a fine introduction to a most important figure in the history of Christian ideas. It will be especially welcomed by those able to read only English, for it is the first general book on Irenaeus to appear in English since 1959.

Brian Davies OP

Preface

When Erasmus published the first edition of *Adversus Haereses* in 1526 he referred to its author as 'my Irenaeus'. He was proud to claim ownership not just because he had restored to light a book that had been virtually forgotten for over a thousand years, but much more because it revealed a picture of the life and thought of the early Church which was markedly and refreshingly different from the life and thought of the Church of his own times. It breathed, he said, the ancient vigour of the Gospel. This was in the letter by which he dedicated the edition to the Bishop of Trent, the city in which the Council of the Counter-Reformation was to meet some nineteen years later. Erasmus hoped that in his own troubled times another Irenaeus might rise up and lead the Church back to peace through the spirit of the Gospel.[1]

Irenaeus has shown no sign of falling back into oblivion. Many editions and translations of his works have appeared and much scholarship has been devoted to them. Most authors writing from within the broad catholic tradition have shared Erasmus' enthusiasm for Irenaeus. Some have gone beyond Erasmus' claim of ownership to contend that others, for confessional purposes, have tried to steal him. Thus, the French Catholic Massuet thought the German Anglican Grabe had tried to make an unwilling and reluctant Anglican of Irenaeus.[2]

While his admirers look to Irenaeus as one of the earliest representatives of the developing catholic tradition and could point to the documents of the Second Vatican Council as witness to the reinvigorating influence of his theology, admiration for him has not been universal. Those who have considered his early catholicism itself to be a perversion of the Gospel, understandably find him less attractive.[3] More recently, Irenaeus has attracted adverse attention as an early advocate of patriarchal forms of church government.[4]

Although scholarly interest in Irenaeus shows no signs of abating, its fruits most frequently appear in languages other than English. There has not been a general monograph on Irenaeus published in English since G. Wingren, *Man and the Incarnation. A Study in the Biblical Theology of Irenaeus* (Edinburgh and London, 1959), itself a translation from Swedish.

The present work aims to be an introduction to the theology of Irenaeus, not an introduction to all the various problems associated with the study of his writings. These are not, as it happens, particularly easy to read. At times, Irenaeus' ideas can seem as quaint and unfamiliar as those of the heretics he routed, and, as so little of what he wrote survives in the language in which he wrote, an educated guess at what the original Greek might have been is often crucial to the interpretation of his thought. Another problem arises from the presence in his writings of seemingly contradictory ideas. An obvious solution to this problem is to suggest that Irenaeus has been influenced by and has at times even quoted without acknowledgement the work of other theologians. Friedrich Loofs discovered several such sources in *Adversus Haereses* and suggested that Irenaeus, far from deserving his reputation as a theologian, was a careless and muddle-headed anthologist.[5] Other scholars will admit the influence of such sources, but take a more benign view of Irenaeus' use of them. Some find in this an indication of an attractive theological pluralism.[6]

That Irenaeus was influenced by theologians other than those he acknowledges, and that he may from time to time have quoted or paraphrased them, seems scarcely worth disputing. We need to recall, however, that Irenaeus was not attempting a systematic synthesis of theology. Antonio Orbe has rightly said that the claim to have been the first systematic theologians must go to the Valentinians, Irenaeus' opponents.[7] Irenaeus himself would have greeted the expectation that he should produce something original with considerable indignation. Original thinking in theology was precisely the source of the problem he sought to address, not by being original himself, but by demonstrating what was the original, universal, unchanging and uncontaminated teaching handed down from the Apostles. In fact, the tradition he drew on for ideas suiting his own immediate purpose was already richly variegated, and it is ironic that Irenaeus himself should unwittingly show us this. He evidently did not notice that the ideas and formulations which he borrowed from different sources were sometimes inconsistent with one another, or contradictory. He took the uniformity of the orthodox tradition for granted, and drew upon its various representatives, in piecemeal fashion, to establish his argument against his opponents.

Irenaeus' principal work was a polemic against contemporary Christians whose theological views, he believed, separated them from the community of believers. His own theology cannot be divorced from this polemical context. One cannot fully understand what he means at any point unless one knows what it is he is arguing against at that point—what is the false teaching which his own teaching is meant to correct. At the beginning of Book V of *Adversus Haereses* he urges his readers to read the previous four books carefully, so that they 'may know what the views are that we are arguing against'. For all this, an introduction to his theology which constantly adverted to its polemical context might soon become tiresome, and obscure the positive and enduring value of the theology which emerged as he elaborated his polemic.

The first chapter of this book provides a brief introduction to Irenaeus' life, background and writings. The second sketches the more significant of the heresies as described by him in Book I. This sketch does not claim to treat these theological systems as adequately as they might deserve, or to take account of the vast amount of scholarly discussion they have occasioned, especially in the wake of the modern discoveries of original gnostic sources.[8] Its function will be simply to explain why Irenaeus' theology took the shape it did.

The third chapter will sample Irenaeus' attempt to show that the heretics' assaults upon the doctrine of the oneness of God cannot withstand a close examination, by reason of their inconsistency, capriciousness and faulty logic. This chapter will draw its material mainly from the stony ground of Book II. The doctrine of the unity of God preoccupies Irenaeus to the end of the whole work. His argument in Books III to V seeks to show that, rightly interpreted, the Scriptures lend no support to the theories of the heretics but, on the contrary, demonstrate that there is only one God who is the creator of the world. It is in this more scriptural and theological section of his work that, by reason of the vigour, charm, and even naïvety of his ideas, Irenaeus has most won and still holds the attention of his readers. It is here that we encounter the development and integration of ideas which single him out as the 'father' of theology, as the writer in whom a relatively clear and full picture of 'early catholicism' first emerges. The remaining chapters of the present work will draw chiefly on these books, and on the *Demonstration of the Apostolic Preaching*.

'Early catholicism' merits a brief explanation. It is a technical term (*Frühkatholizismus*) which, J. D. G. Dunn says, 'seems to have been coined round about the turn of the century. But the issues involved in it go back at least to the middle of the nineteenth century and the Tübingen school of F. C. Baur.'[9] The term is meant to indicate the synthesis forged in the early Church between conflicting views, such as Judaeo-Christianity on the one hand, and Pauline Christianity on the other. Its Hegelian premise might be open to challenge, but it is a convenient way to acknowledge that the Christianity represented by Irenaeus is recognizably that of the Catholic Church, and yet unfamiliar in its primitiveness. F. Mussner gives the following among the characteristics of *Frühkatholizismus*: a hierarchical, instead of a simply charismatic, structure of the Church, the development of a monarchical episcopacy, a strictly defined Rule of Faith, the principle of succession, the distinction between priests and laity, an authoritative interpretation of Scripture, sacramentalism, a 'naturalistic' theology, and so on.[10] In Irenaeus' writings some of these characteristics are more marked than others.

Another technical term, also of German origin, of which I have made use is the 'Great Church' (*Grosskirche*). This term is usually applied to the mainstream Christian Church between AD 180 and 333.[11] Chronologically, Irenaeus barely qualifies for inclusion in it. I have used it, for want of a better term, to indicate, with as little prejudice as possible, the ecclesial community dispersed throughout the Mediterranean world to which Irenaeus belonged, which he regarded as authentic, and from which he therefore proposed to exclude the heretics.

Quotations from Scripture are in the Revised Standard Version, Catholic Edition, published by the Catholic Truth Society, London. Translations in other quotations, unless otherwise indicated, are my own.

The reader should be aware that I wrote a doctoral dissertation at the University of Oxford, 1980–84, largely concerned with the writings of Irenaeus. Doctoral research involves one in close analysis of the work of other scholars, leading sometimes to agreement and sometimes to disagreement, but always to a sharing in a broad consensus, in which it is often difficult to recall the particular contributions of different scholars. While I hope my interpretation has taken contemporary scholarship adequately into account, I have thought it better not to clutter this introductory book with the details of often recondite scholarly debates about the interpretation of Irenaeus' works. This approach makes sense in an introduction to almost any ancient author, but it has special point in the case of Irenaeus, since his writings are known, in the main, only by way of translations into Latin, Armenian, and Syriac, and no complete, serviceable translation into English, incorporating the results of modern scholarship, is yet available.[12] With this book I hope to make Irenaeus' theology reasonably accessible to the English reader, and, perhaps, to provoke the reader to undertake the rather daunting task of launching into the study of Irenaeus' writings. If I succeed in this, my success will be due to the clarity of vision I have gained from the work of others and I here acknowledge my debt to them in a general way, without, of course, implicating them in my own errors of judgement or interpretation.

Maurice Wiles guided my first explorations in Irenaeus' theology. Paul Parvis OP uncomplainingly endured countless discussions of the subject. Philip Kennedy OP read a draft of this book at short notice and made valuable suggestions. None may be held responsible for any folly remaining in these pages. Brian Davies OP has shown that *makrothumia* is not a virtue confined to the Godhead.

Denis Minns OP

28 June 1993

Feast of St Irenaeus of Lyons

Notes

1 D. Erasmus (ed.), *Opus eruditissimum Divi Irenaei* (Basle, 1526), pp. 2–3.

2 R. Massuet (ed.), *Sancti Irenaei . . . Opera* (Paris, 1710), pp. vi–vii.

3 J. Werner judged that, for all his quotation and discussion of Paul, Irenaeus missed the central issues of Paul's theology: *Der Paulinismus des Irenäus. Eine Kirchen- und Dogmengeschichtliche Untersuchung über das Verhaltnis des Irenäus zur Paulinischen Briefsammlung und Theologie* (Texte und Untersuchungen 6.2; 1889). Barbara Aland offers a far more sympathetic reading of Irenaeus from within the Lutheran tradition: 'Fides und Subjectio. Zur Anthropologie des Irenäus' in Adolf Martin Ritter (ed.), *Kerygma und Logos. Beiträge zu den geistesgeschichtlichen Beziehungen zwischen Antike*

und Christentum. Festschrift für Carl Andresen zum 70. Geburtstag (Göttingen, 1979), pp. 9–28.

4   E. Pagels, *The Gnostic Gospels* (Penguin Books, 1982), pp. 80ff. and 'The Demiurge and his Archons. A Gnostic view of the bishop and presbyters?', *Harvard Theological Review* 69 (1976), pp. 301–24 (pp. 320ff.).

5   F. Loofs, *Theophilus von Antiochien Adversus Marcionem und die anderen theologischen Quellen bei Irenaeus* (Texte und Untersuchungen 46.2; 1930), p. 432.

6   Thus Martin Widmann, 'Irenäus und seine theologischen Väter', *Zeitschrift für Theologie und Kirche* 54 (1957), pp. 156–73 (p. 172).

7   E.g. A. Orbe, *Teología de San Ireneo. Comentario al Libro V del 'Adversus haereses'* I (Biblioteca de Autores Cristianos; Madrid, 1985), p. 9. Adolf Harnack had said the gnostics were 'the Theologians of the first century . . . the first to transform Christianity into a system of doctrines': *History of Dogma* I, trans. Neil Buchanan (London, 1905), p. 228.

8   G. Filoramo, *A History of Gnosticism*, trans. A. Alcock (Oxford: Basil Blackwell, 1990) is an excellent discussion, taking full account of the Nag Hammadi find.

9   J. D. G. Dunn, *Unity and Diversity in the New Testament: An Inquiry into the Character of Earliest Christianity* (London, 1977), p. 341.

10 F. Mussner in *Lexikon für Theologie und Kirche* 6, ed. J. Höfer and K. Rahner (Freiburg, 1961), col. 89.

11 H. Rahner in *Lexikon für Theologie und Kirche* 4, ed. J. Höfer and K. Rahner (Freiburg, 1960), col. 413, places Irenaeus in a first period of church history, which he calls the 'church of the origins' (*Urkirche*).

12 The first volume of a new translation of *Adversus Haereses* appeared in 1992, translated and annotated by Dominic J. Unger, with further revision by John J. Dillon (Ancient Christian Writers 55; New York). I have not been able to make use of it here.

Bibliography

THE WORKS OF IRENAEUS
Editions

Adversus Haereses
The first printed edition was that published by Erasmus at Basle in 1526. The most recent is that published in the series Sources chrétiennes (SC) between 1952 and 1982. This is a full critical edition of the Latin text and Greek fragments, accompanied by an indication of significant variants in the Syriac and Armenian fragments, a French translation and five volumes of introduction and textual commentary.

Contre les hérésies, livre I, édition critique par A. Rousseau et L. Doutreleau (SC 263–264; 2 vols, Paris, 1979).

Contre les hérésies, livre II, édition critique par A. Rousseau et L. Doutreleau (SC 293–294; 2 vols, Paris, 1982).

Contre les hérésies, livre III, édition critique par A. Rousseau et L. Doutreleau (SC 210–211; 2 vols, Paris, 1974). This replaces an earlier edition of Book III by F. Sagnard (SC 34, Paris, 1952).

Contre les hérésies, livre IV, édition critique d'après les versions arménienne et latine, sous la direction de A. Rousseau, avec la collaboration de B. Hemmerdinger, L. Doutreleau, C. Mercier (SC 100; 2 vols, Paris, 1979).

Contre les hérésies, livre V, édition critique d'après les versions arménienne et latine, par A. Rousseau, L. Doutreleau, C. Mercier (SC 152–153; 2 vols, Paris, 1969).

Earlier editions of *Adversus Haereses* often reward consultation, especially those of J. E. Grabe (Oxford, 1702), R. Massuet (Paris, 1710; reprinted in J. P. Migne, Patrologia Graeca 7, Paris, 1857) and W. W. Harvey (Cambridge, 1857).

The Demonstration of the Apostolic Preaching
Des heiligen Irenäus Schrift zum Erweise der apostolischen Verkündigung . . . in armenischer Version entdeckt und ins Deutsche übersetzt von K. Mekerttschian und E. Minassiantz, mit einem Nachwort und Anmerkungen von A. Harnack (Texte und Untersuchungen 31.1; Leipzig, 1907).
The Proof of the Apostolic Preaching, with seven fragments, Armenian version edited and translated by K. Mekerttschian and S. G. Wilson (Patrologia Orientalis 12.5; Paris, 1919).

English translations

Adversus Haereses
Five Books of S. Irenaeus, Bishop of Lyons, Against Heresies, translated by J. Keble (London, 1872).
The Writings of Irenaeus, translated by A. Roberts and W. H. Rambaut (The Ante-Nicene Fathers, 2 vols, Edinburgh, 1868–69; reprinted by W. B. Eerdmans: Michigan, 1979).

The Demonstration of the Apostolic Preaching
The Demonstration of the Apostolic Preaching, translated from the Armenian with introduction and notes by J. A. Robinson (London, 1920).
Proof of the Apostolic Preaching, translated and annotated by J. P. Smith (Ancient Christian Writers 16; London and New York, 1952).

OTHER AUTHORS

There is a huge bibliography for Irenaeus. The following is restricted to monographs and, with the exception of English titles, to those published in the last 40 years.

Y. de Andia, *Homo vivens. Incorruptibilité et divinisation de l'homme selon Irénée de Lyon* (Paris, 1986).
P. Bacq, *De l'ancienne à la nouvelle Alliance selon S. Irénée* (Paris, 1978).

A. Bengsch, *Heilsgeschichte und Heilswissen. Eine Untersuchung zur Struktur und Entfaltung des theologischen Denkens im Werk Adversus Haereses des hl. Irenäus von Lyon* (Leipzig, 1957).

A. Benoît, *Saint Irénée. Introduction à l'étude de sa théologie* (Paris, 1960).

R. Berthouzoz, *Liberté et Grâce suivant la théologie d'Irénée de Lyon. Le débat avec la gnose aux origines de la théologie chrétienne* (Fribourg, 1980).

N. Brox, *Offenbarung, Gnosis und gnostischer Mythos bei Irenäus von Lyon. Zur Charakteristik der System* (Munich, 1966).

J. Fantino, *L'homme image de Dieu selon saint Irénée de Lyon* (Paris, 1986).

F. R. Montgomery Hitchcock, *Irenaeus of Lugdunum: A Study of His Teaching* (Cambridge, 1914).

H.-J. Jaschke, *Der Heilige Geist im Bekenntnis der Kirche. Eine Studie zur Pneumatologie des Irenäus von Lyon im Ausgang vom altchristlichen Glaubensbekenntnis* (Münster, 1976).

G. Joppich, *Salus Carnis. Eine Untersuchung in der Theologie des hl. Irenäus von Lyon* (Münsterschwarzach, 1965).

H. Lassiat, *Promotion de l'homme en Jésus Christ d'après Irénée de Lyon. Témoin de la tradition des Apôtres* (Paris, 1974).

J. Lawson, *The Biblical Theology of Saint Irenaeus* (London, 1948).

A. Orbe, *Antropología de San Ireneo* (Madrid, 1969).

A. Orbe, *Parábolas Evangélicas en San Ireneo* (2 vols, Madrid, 1972).

A. Orbe, *Teología de San Ireneo. Comentario al Libro V del 'Adversus haereses'* (3 vols, Madrid, 1985, 1987, 1988).

A. Orbe, *Espiritualidad de San Ireneo* (Rome, 1989).

R. Tremblay, *La manifestation et la vision de Dieu selon saint Irénée de Lyon* (Münster, 1978).

G. Wingren, *Man and the Incarnation. A Study in the Biblical Theology of Irenaeus*, translated by R. Mackenzie (Edinburgh and London, 1959).

ABBREVIATIONS

AH *Adversus Haereses*
Dem *Demonstration of the Apostolic Preaching*
SC *Sources chrétiennes*

1

Introduction

THE LIFE OF IRENAEUS

Very little is known of the life of Irenaeus. He tells us that in his youth he had heard Polycarp preach, and the memory remained vivid for him.[1] As Polycarp was Bishop of Smyrna (Izmir, in what is now Turkey) and was martyred there, most probably in the latter half of the 150s,[2] it is generally assumed that Irenaeus was himself a native of Asia Minor, if not of Smyrna itself.[3] His language was Greek, and his style makes it clear that he received more than a rudimentary education. Pierre Nautin has suggested that he may have gone from Asia Minor to Rome in pursuit of a career in rhetoric, and from there moved to Gaul.[4]

In 177, according to Eusebius' *Church History*, the Christian communities of Lyons and Vienne were subjected to a fierce persecution.[5] Eusebius tells us that they made public

> various letters of martyrs who had been perfected among them, which they had written, while still in chains, to the brothers in Asia and Phrygia, and also to Eleutherius, who was then bishop of the Romans, making representations for the sake of the peace of the churches.[6]

Eusebius quotes part of the letter to Eleutherius, in which Irenaeus is introduced as the bearer of the letter and a presbyter of the Church. In some Christian communities, at least, the words 'presbyter' and 'bishop' had been used interchangeably, and it is

1

possible that Irenaeus himself does not recognize much of a distinction between them.[7] His own status at this time was probably closer to what Eusebius (and we) would call 'bishop' than to 'priest', but whether he exercised this office alone, or as a member of a college of elders and overseers (which is what the words 'presbyter' and 'bishop' mean) may be doubted. In any case, it might seem odd that a high official in the Christian community should not only be at liberty while other members of that community were imprisoned, but even be able to travel to Rome on the business of the community. Pierre Nautin has proposed that Irenaeus had been bishop of the Christian community at Vienne, not far distant from Lyons, and that when Pothinus, Bishop of Lyons, died in prison during the persecution, he assumed episcopal authority over the Christians in both cities.[8] This is a possibility, but it needs to be borne in mind that Irenaeus himself nowhere lays claim to being a bishop.[9]

Eleutherius was Bishop of Rome between about 174 and 189, when he was succeeded by Victor, who reigned until 198. Eusebius tells us that Irenaeus wrote 'on behalf of the brothers in Gaul, of whom he was leader', reprimanding Victor for attempting to bully the churches of Asia Minor into following the date favoured by the Roman church for the celebration of Easter.[10]

There is no evidence that Irenaeus lived beyond the reign of Victor. He is commemorated as a martyr, but evidence that he died a martyr's death is slight and unconvincing.[11]

THE CHURCHES OF VIENNE AND LYONS

Although we know so little about Irenaeus, we have an invaluable insight into his Christian milieu through the letter addressed by the churches of Vienne and Lyons to the churches of Asia and Phrygia, describing the persecution they had recently undergone. The letter was written in Greek, and it is possible, as Nautin argues, that Irenaeus drafted it.[12] Greek was the language of the Christian communities in Asia Minor to whom the letter was addressed. It was probably also the everyday language of most of the Christians of Lyons and Vienne, just as it was of the Christians of Rome at this time.[13] It is reasonable to suppose that many of the Christians of Lyons and Vienne had their origins in the Eastern part of the Empire.[14] Latin names occur alongside Greek ones in the letter, and the deacon Sanctus is said to have addressed the tribunal in

Latin. Irenaeus was to excuse his own literary style on the ground that he had lived amongst the Celts and had had to do a lot of talking in a barbarous tongue (AH I.praef.3).

In the substantial portions of the letter which Eusebius preserves we are able to glimpse a remarkable Christian community, proud of those members who had endured appalling torments, but prepared to acknowledge that some had weakened and, what was even more unusual in the early Church, prepared to forgive them. Although we hear of the aged bishop Pothinus, and of Sanctus, a deacon from Vienne, there is very little indication of a sharp distinction between clergy and laity. Indeed, Pothinus and Sanctus are the only persons identified as holding ecclesiastical office. While several other martyrs are named, and their torments described, there can be little doubt that the central hero of this narrative is the slave Blandina.

In the martyr-literature of the early Church the notions of union between the martyr and Christ, of the martyr's imitation of Christ, and of Christ suffering in the martyr, are very prominent. They are developed to a high degree, for example, in the account of the martyrdom of Polycarp.[15] That record presents the bishop Polycarp, and him alone, as identified with Christ in martyrdom, despite the fact that others were martyred with him. In the letter of the churches of Vienne and Lyons it is Blandina who is singled out as especially Christlike. Indeed, she becomes an icon of Christ for those who suffer with her:

> Blandina was hung up on a beam and presented as food for the wild beasts which were set against her. This woman, by being seen hanging in the form of a cross and by her vigorous prayers, caused great eagerness in those who were struggling for the prize. For, thanks to their sister, they were able in their struggle to see, even with their outward eyes, the one who was crucified for them, in order that he might persuade those who believe in him that everyone who suffers for the glory of Christ has for ever fellowship with the living God. She would urge on her brothers, this tiny, weak and easily ignored woman, for she had put on Christ, the great and unconquerable athlete, and had routed her adversary in many bouts and had, on account of her contest, been crowned with the crown of incorruptibility.[16]

It is possible that the Christians of Lyons were conscious that the broader church was undergoing changes which would lead to a more stratified, hierarchical organization. They certainly seem to have been aware that status was more important in the Roman church than in their own. The letter they addressed to Eleutherius contains a polite, but unmistakeable repudiation of the new, emerging order:

> We pray always that you rejoice in God in all things, Father Eleutherius. We have urged our brother and companion Irenaeus to carry these letters to you and we beg you to hold him in commendation as one who is zealous for the covenant of Christ. We would have commended him in the first instance as a presbyter of the Church, which indeed he is, if we knew that place could secure righteousness for anyone.[17]

Irenaeus himself will say of those deemed by the multitude to be presbyters but who are enslaved to their own pleasures and do not give prime place in their hearts to the fear of God, treating everyone else with contempt, puffed up with pride in their presidential seats, doing evil in secret while imagining no one sees them, that they will receive their rebuke from the Word, who judges not according to opinion, or according to outward appearance, but according to what is in the heart (AH IV.26.3).

Lyons, once one of the most prosperous cities in the Western part of the Empire, fell into decline at about the turn of the second century, possibly as a result of a sack after Septimius Severus defeated his rival emperor, Clodius Albinus, near the city in 197. We hear no more of the Greek-speaking Christian community of Lyons after this.

THE WORKS OF IRENAEUS

Of the several works of Irenaeus mentioned by Eusebius only two survive complete, neither of them in Irenaeus' Greek.[18] Although Irenaeus has often been described as the father or founder of Catholic theology, the development of theology in the centuries after his death was such that many of his views must very soon have appeared old-fashioned. Tertullian, writing within a decade or two of Irenaeus, speaks as though interest in him was largely antiquarian.[19] The two works which have survived this neglect are *The Detection and Overthrow of So-called Knowledge*, most often known as *Adversus Haereses* (*Against the Heresies*), and *The Demonstration of the Apostolic Preaching*. *Adversus Haereses* survives almost complete in a Latin translation, the date of which has been much disputed. It is certainly earlier than 421 in which year Augustine quoted from it.[20] The manuscripts of this Latin version demonstrate how hazardous was the survival of an ancient work until the invention of the printing press, especially if it contained theological views no longer current, or of doubtful orthodoxy. *Adversus Haereses* concludes with a discussion of the kingdom of Christ which clearly understands it to be a this-worldly reality, of lengthy but finite duration. Only one of the Latin manuscripts preserves this section, and even it omits a small but crucial paragraph.

All five books of *Adversus Haereses* were translated into Armenian. This translation has been variously dated between the first half of the fifth century and the first half of the eighth. Fragments of the first three books and a complete text of Books IV and V survive in this translation. It is thanks to this Armenian version that we know that even the most complete of the Latin manuscripts omitted a section of the text. The Greek text of parts of *Adversus Haereses* can be known from quotations in other authors and from a couple of short papyrus fragments. Quotations also survive in other languages, most notably in Syriac. The best edition of *Adversus Haereses* is that published in the series Sources chrétiennes, details of which will be found in the Bibliography. The most accessible English translation at present is that of A. Roberts and W. H. Rambaut.

The Demonstration of the Apostolic Preaching, which was known to Eusebius, survives only in an Armenian translation, discovered in 1904 and published for the first time in 1907. This short 'manual of essentials', addressed to a certain Marcianus, is by far the simpler of the two surviving works. Although it was written after *Adversus Haereses*, to which it refers, and is meant to assist in the fight against false teaching, it has almost none of the polemical tone of the larger work and often suggests a more primitive theology, unrefined by the conflict with heresy (Dem 1; 99). After a brief exhortation to the reader to combine bodily holiness with adherence to the truth faith (1–2) the *Demonstration* may be divided into two main sections. In the first (3–42), Irenaeus sets out the central tenets of the Rule of Faith: that there is one God who is Father, Son and Spirit, who created everything, and created humankind to have dominion over everything on the earth; and that, after the Fall, God continued his saving purpose for humankind through the history recorded in the Old Testament which reached its culmination in the life and death of Jesus, who undid the disobedience of Adam, fulfilled the promises made to the patriarchs, and, by the preaching of the Apostles, made the Gentile Church heir to those promises. In the second part (42–97), Irenaeus seeks to demonstrate the truth of the principal claims of the first part by the quotation, interpretation, and application of proof texts from the Old Testament prophets. The claims made for Christ and his work, Irenaeus says, are difficult enough to believe in themselves. They are credible because they were foretold by God through the prophets and then brought to reality by him just as had been foretold (Dem 42).

There are scholarly English translations of the *Demonstration* by J. A. Robinson and J. P. Smith.[21]

Adversus Haereses consists of two very unequal parts. The first book is the detection, or uncovering, of heresy. Here Irenaeus sets out what he believes to be the views of the heretics he opposes. The overthrowing of these heretical views, which commences with Book II, itself has two parts. Book II engages with the heresies outlined in Book I and attempts to show their lack of foundation in reason or revelation. The remaining books argue from Scripture against the heretical theses, sometimes shared by various schools, which Irenaeus considers most pernicious.

Irenaeus' claims, at the beginning of *Adversus Haereses*, not to have studied rhetoric, or the 'art of words', and to be unaccustomed to literary composition, themselves probably have a rhetorical origin.[22] Irenaeus had much more than a nodding acquaintance with the techniques of rhetoric, as his preference for long, complicated, and carefully balanced sentences makes plain. But this should not obscure from us the fact that *Adversus Haereses* was written out of a pressing sense of pastoral need (AH I.praef.; V.praef.), and that Irenaeus several times changed his mind about the length and scope of the work. He seems, at times, distinctly embarrassed at the way the project has escaped from his original plan, and at his consequent prolixity.[23]

It is clear from the preface to Book III that the first two books were originally intended to meet the title of the whole as 'The Detection and Overthrow of Knowledge Falsely So-Called'. Book I uncovers and exposes the heresies by describing them in some detail and showing their ultimate dependence on the errors of Simon the Magician. Book II overthrows these errors by pointing up their inherent inconsistencies and weaknesses. At the end of Book I Irenaeus was confident, now that the opinions of the heretics had been exposed to public view, that there would not be much need of further discourse to overturn them (AH I.31.4). The first two books had already been sent to the friend who requested them when Irenaeus was writing Book III. He had evidently become more sharply aware in the course of writing Books I and II of something already noticed at the beginning of the first: that his opponents considered themselves to be the rightful owners and authentic interpreters of the same Scriptures which he and his Church regarded as normative. Hence, at the end of Book II, he foreshadows a third book which will leave aside the dreary reportage of the first and tortuous refutation of the second and show that the Scriptures themselves actually contain a much more open and accessible demonstration of the truths he has been trying to prove — at least for those who do not interpret them perversely (AH II.35.4). In the preface to Book III his confidence is still strong that this book will complete the exercise:

> add this to the earlier two and you will have from us a complete argument against all the heretics and you will be able faithfully and immediately to contend against them for the sake of the only true and life-giving faith, which the Church received from the Apostles and hands on to her children.

By the end of Book III he finds that he has by no means exhausted the potential of the Scriptures as an arsenal against the heretics, and promises a fourth book which will confine itself to arguments drawn from the recorded utterances of Christ. With the completion of Book IV, by far the longest of the five, Irenaeus finds that he has been dealing almost exclusively with the parables of Christ. A fifth book is therefore indicated, which will draw upon the straightforward, non-parabolic, utterances of Christ, and which will also concern itself with the letters of Paul, especially in so far as these have been misinterpreted by the heretics (AH IV.41.4).

In some of the Latin manuscripts, each of Books I to IV is preceded by a list of headings, and the books are divided into chapters. Book V has no list of headings, nor is it divided into chapters. Subsequent editors have devised their own division of chapters and sub-divisions of chapters within each of the five books, frequently in disagreement with one another. Purely for reasons of convenience, and despite its inadequacies, the division and numbering adopted by Massuet has become standard, and is adopted here.

The structure of a literary work was much more important and obvious to ancient authors and readers than it is likely to be to most modern readers. In longer and complicated works the structure can often be quite intricate, and this is certainly the case with Irenaeus' *Adversus Haereses*. Readers of that work may find the task more congenial if they allow themselves to be guided by one or another of the detailed discussions of its literary structure which are available.[24]

Notes

1 AH III.3.4, and Eusebius, *Church History* V.20.6.

2 T. D. Barnes, 'Pre-Decian Acta Martyrum', *Journal of Theological Studies* 19 (1968), pp. 509–31 (p. 512).

3 Thus Pierre Nautin, *Lettres et écrivains chrétiens des IIe et IIIe Siècles* (Paris, 1961), p. 92.

4 *Lettres et écrivains*, p. 93.

5 This date is not absolutely secure: cf. Barnes, 'Pre-Decian Acta Martyrum', pp. 518–19; Nautin, *Lettres et écrivains*, pp. 62–5.

6 Eusebius, *Church History* V.3.4.

7 Cf. *1 Clement* 44.4–5.

8 *Lettres et écrivains*, p. 94.

9 At AH V.praef. Irenaeus tells us that he has been appointed to the service of the Word, and at II.17.1 that he has been given the task of investigating the theories of the gnostics.

10 Eusebius, *Church History* V.24.11–17.

11 In Jerome's *Commentary on Isaiah* Irenaeus is described as 'Bishop of Lyons *and martyr*'; *In Esaiam* XVII, Is 64:4–5 (Corpus Christianorum 83). Henry Dodwell suggested that this was due to a scribal gloss, for when Jerome refers to Irenaeus elsewhere he never describes him as a martyr, and nor do any other ancient Christian writers, even in contexts where such a reference would be highly relevant: *Dissertationes in Irenaeum* (Oxford, 1689), pp. 264 and 259ff. Irenaeus' martyrdom is first reported by Gregory of Tours (d. 594), *Historia Francorum* I.27 (Patrologia Latina 71, cols 174–5).

12 *Lettres et écrivains*, pp. 54–61.

13 Victor may have been the first Bishop of Rome whose native language was Latin.

14 The letter itself mentions two such: Attalus, from Pergamum, and Alexander, from Phrygia.

15 'The Martyrdom of St Polycarp' in Herbert Musurillo (ed.), *The Acts of the Christian Martyrs* (Oxford, 1972), pp. 2–21.

16 'The Martyrs of Lyons', *Acts of the Christian Martyrs*, p. 75 (=Eusebius, *Church History* V.1.41–42; my translation).

17 Eusebius, *Church History* V.4.2.

18 Eusebius, *Church History* V.20; 24.11–18; 26.

19 Tertullian, *Adversus Valentinianos* 5.1.

20 Augustine, *Contra Iulianum* I.3.5 (Patrologia Latina 44, col. 644).

21 Smith's translation omits a small but significant phrase at Dem 88 ('And that he was Himself to bring about these blessings in person *and that he would redeem us by his own blood*, Isaias declared in the words . . .'). Robinson omits a less significant phrase at Dem 19 ('. . . being shut up in the ark *with all the animals which God ordered Noah to bring into the ark*'). *La prédication des apôtres et ses preuves ou la foi chrétienne*, trans. J. Bartholout, rev. (based on original) S. Voïcou, introduction and notes A. G. Hamman (Les Pères dans la Foi; Desclée de Brouwer, 1977) omits a significant passage from Dem 31, disturbs the order of Dem 62–67, and is often loose in the translation. The invaluable Latin translation of Simon Weber (*Sancti Irenaei . . . Demonstratio Apostolicae Praedicationis*, Freiburg, 1917) was intended to represent the Armenian as closely as possible.

22 AH I.praef.2, 3. Cf. W. R. Schoedel, 'Philosophy and rhetoric in the *Adversus Haereses* of Irenaeus', *Vigiliae Christianae* 13 (1959), pp. 22–32 (p. 27).

23 E.g. AH III.12.9.

24 See A. Benoît, *Saint Irénée. Introduction à l'étude de sa théologie* (Paris, 1960); P. Bacq, *De l'ancienne à la nouvelle alliance selon S. Irénée. Unité du Livre IV de l'"Adversus Haereses'* (Paris, 1978); and the companion volumes of the Sources chrétiennes edition of *Adversus Haereses*.

9

2

Heresies

INTRODUCTION

'Heresy' is derived from a Greek word meaning 'choice'. It came to be used in a quite neutral sense of a group of people who chose to adhere to a particular set of philosophical or religious teachings. In the New Testament the word is used in this neutral sense of the Sadducees (Acts 5:17), and the Pharisees (Acts 15:5; 26:5). A party within a larger organization can easily come to see itself, or be seen by others, as exclusive. Then the word *hairesis* can have a pejorative tone, as it probably does when used of Christians at Acts 24:5 and 28:22. When exclusiveness is perceived as leading to rupture from the larger body, heresy is called schism, as at 1 Corinthians 11:18-19, and the word is then used in an entirely pejorative sense (cf. Gal 5:20; 2 Pet 2:1).

Diversity of opinion on important theological issues has existed in the Christian Church from the very beginning. It has not always led to schismatic heresy, and, when it has, it is often difficult to decide whether the decisive break, or schism, has been made by the 'school' which no longer wished to have formal association with the larger parent body, or by the larger body which decided that association with the 'school' was no longer tolerable. To speak, as I have just done, of 'the larger group' already betrays a certain prejudice. It is a very old prejudice, which was already establishing itself at the time Irenaeus was writing. It is the prejudice of supposing that orthodoxy, or right belief, is identical with the majority opinion.

We should remember, however, that it was only at the time of

Irenaeus, and in consequence of the crisis of Marcion and the gnostics, that the orthodox consensus, the majority view, or, as it is often called, the Great Church, came into existence. It is difficult to read Irenaeus and not take him at his own evaluation: difficult not to believe that he is the spokesman of a recognizable body of believers clearly defined by their unanimous acceptance of a set of doctrines held in continuity from the time of the Apostles and in communion with the majority of Christian communities in other places. Equally, it is difficult to disbelieve his suggestion that his opponents cohered in various recognizable sects or schools. In this book I have presumed that there was a reality corresponding to the term 'the Great Church', and that, by and large, Irenaeus represents it. This is a convenient simplification, but a simplification none the less. If we can speak of a 'Great Church' at all, this is at least partly because polemical theologians like Irenaeus identified certain views as incompatible with Christian truth and declared those who held them to be beyond Christian fellowship. Often, this was a thoroughly sensible line to take. There seems, even now, little point in worshipping the Creator of all material things as good, all-powerful, provident and beneficent, alongside someone who despises this creator as an ignorant and vindictive tyrant whose power is relative and limited. Not to exclude the heretics from the Church, Irenaeus argued, would damage its mission. Non-Christians would suppose that they were representative of Christianity, and turn their ears away from the proclamation of the truth (AH I.25.3).

Nevertheless, there was a plurality and diversity of views even within communities which Irenaeus would have regarded as belonging to the authentic Church. Sometimes, tensions arose between those who held contrasting opinions, and battle was joined until the opinion held by one side was declared erroneous, and those who persisted in holding it, heretical.

Gnosticism and Marcionism apart, most of the great heresies of the early Church were survivals of opinions which, prior to the declaration of heresy, had been fully at home and widely held within the mainstream Christian community. Some of the heretics described by Irenaeus indignantly disputed their exclusion from the Church. Even if they met together apart from the main body of the Church (AH IV.26.2), they claimed that they belonged within the mainstream community: their difference, they said, was that they had a more sophisticated, more spiritual, insight into the realities which more simple Christians acknowledged by faith (AH

11

III.15.2). In the third century, Origen would make similar claims for his own approach to theology,[1] and another century would pass before his claim to be the outstanding theologian of the Church would be shamefully subverted, sometimes by those, like Jerome, who had derived most of their own theological training from his writings. Even in Irenaeus, we occasionally find ideas which look to us as though they would be more comfortable in a gnostic setting. No doubt, he thought the business of separating false teaching from the truth was a simple, clear-cut matter. Sometimes it was. To worship a God other than the one revealed in the Old Testament was plainly discontinuous with the religion of Jesus, his disciples, and their earliest followers. At other times, 'the truth' was only just coming to be recognized as such, and it was in the very act of recognizing it that the Great Church came into being.

Those who took upon themselves the task of identifying and over-throwing heresy soon developed an armoury of weapons to be used against false teaching. Some of these have had a long history and are still influential today. We need to be conscious of them, and cautious of their influence. Among them are the notions that 'heresy' is always a subsequent perversion of the original truth; that it is a minority view; that its propagators were motivated by malice, immorality, or disappointment of holding high office in the Great Church; that heresies gave rise to one another, so that one can plot them all on a genealogical tree. Sometimes quite commonplace prejudices were called into play. There was no easier way to damn a theologian in the ancient Church than to say that he came from Libya. One further prejudice, embedded in the way the opinions of the gnostics have come down to us, should be mentioned here. It was a standard tactic of anti-heretical polemic in the early Church to accuse the heretics of aiming to 'capture weak women, burdened with sins and swayed by various impulses, who will listen to anybody and can never arrive at a knowledge of the truth' (2 Tim 3:6–7). Irenaeus says the gnostics put this strategy to good effect in his own region by the Rhône (AH I.13.7). We can form something of an impression of the appeal that gnosticism might have had for women in the second century, but we cannot form that impression on the basis of what those women themselves thought and felt. Their voices have not survived.

In recent times, awareness of these prejudices has meant a somewhat fairer hearing for ancient heresies. They labour under a greater disability, however, which can seldom if ever be overcome. For the most part, our knowledge of ancient heresies must come to us through the filter of the Great Church. Rarely do we have whole works of heretical writers. Such fragments as still exist have survived because they have been quoted, to suit their own purposes, by anti-heretical polemicists. This was largely the case with the gnostics until the discovery, in 1945, at Nag Hammadi in Egypt, of a library of 52 mainly gnostic writings.[2] While many of these writings derive from the same gnostic schools which Irenaeus combated, they offer a significantly different picture of gnostic doctrines from that which he presents. Inevitably, this has given rise to controversy about how accurately Irenaeus represented gnostic doctrines. Fortunately, we do not need to enter into this argument here. Irenaeus believed the picture of the gnostics which he presented to be an accurate one. A doctor, he says in extenuation of his lengthy recital of gnostic doctrines in Book I, cannot cure a disease if he does not know what it is (AH IV.praef.2). Other gnostic ideas may well have influenced him, directly or indirectly, and even been welcomed. It is certain that the picture he offers of gnostic teachings is far from complete. Nevertheless, he elaborated his theology chiefly in opposition to what he supposed the heretical views to be. For this reason, the brief outline of heresies which follows will draw principally on Irenaeus' own description, and especially on the description of the school of Valentinus with which he begins his account. Valentinus was born in Egypt and educated at Alexandria. By the middle years of the second century he was teaching in Rome, where he was a prominent member of the Christian community. He was a remarkably inventive theologian and, along with Marcion, among the chief glories of that golden age of Roman theology.

GNOSTICISM

The theologians whom Irenaeus opposes are sometimes lumped together under the omnibus term 'gnostics' and their ideas under the term 'gnosticism'. This is a modern usage, and it is not accurate. It does, however, have a limited convenience, and it is partly founded upon Irenaeus' own way of dealing with the heretical schools in Book I. The usage is not accurate because it extends to all the heterodox theologians described by Irenaeus a title which appears to have been peculiar to a number of specific sects. The *gnōstikoi* do not make their appearance until the very end of Book I, and, even then, they are hardly represented as holding a coherent and consistent set of doctrines. Irenaeus speaks of them as a multitude

springing up like mushrooms, and he goes on to outline two distinctive sets of teachings associated with them.[3] These 'gnostics' are
identified by Irenaeus as the immediate forerunners of the school
of Valentinus,[4] his primary target, the description of which opens
the first book of *Adversus Haereses*. Nor is it only between these
'gnostics' and the Valentinians that he discerns such a link. All the
heretics, he claims, succeed one another in a line stretching back
to Simon Magus, who made a brief appearance in Acts 8, and was
accorded a highly coloured subsequent career in the Christian tradition.[5] For all the variety of sects described in Book I, it remains the
case that Irenaeus' target throughout the work is, as he says in his
title, 'gnosis falsely so-called'. The term 'gnosticism' has come to be
used widely of a number of philosophical–religious world-views,
dating from the late first or second century, which placed knowledge, as opposed to faith, at the centre of religious experience. In
this book the term 'gnostic' is used loosely to indicate both these
views and those who held them.

In the schools described by Irenaeus, *gnōsis* is knowledge about
the divine realm, about the creation and nature of the world and of
humankind, about sin, suffering and evil, and about redemption.
Possession of this knowledge is salvation. This knowledge is not
attained by observation or by rational argument, but by revelation:
revelation which is not *believed*, but *known* to be true. Although the
content of this knowledge embraces everything, the central object of
knowledge is the gnostic's own self: all other dimensions of the
knowledge are peripheral to and supportive of this. The gnostic
knows himself or herself to be, in his or her essential and highest
part, divine. To have this knowledge is already to be saved. Nevertheless, the gnostic must await the final separation of the divine
element from matter so that it can return to the divine realm. Not
everybody has this knowledge, because not everybody has the divine
element which is capable of knowing itself to be divine. For there
are three classes of human beings. Only the gnostics possess the
divine, spiritual spark. Another class is made up of those who do not
have the divine spirit, but do have souls. These are not capable
of knowledge, but they are capable of faith. Human beings of a
third class have neither divine spirit nor soul. They are merely
matter, and their only end is corruption. The gnostics described
these three classes of human beings as 'pneumatic' (spiritual),
'psychic' (ensouled) and 'hylic' (material) (AH I.5.1 – 6.2).

Although at present trapped in matter, the spiritual know that the
divine element in them will eventually and naturally return to the

14

divine realm. Leading a moral life is not a condition for this return, which will happen by necessity of nature. The psychics are placed between the spiritual and the material and have the capacity to incline toward either. This capacity is free will. If they incline towards the material they will eventually crumble away to nothing. Although they cannot attain the same salvation as the spiritual, if by free will they incline toward the spiritual, they will be rewarded in a garden of rest after death.[6] The gnostics classed the great majority of Christian believers among the psychics (AH I.6.2).

This doctrine of the three classes of human beings is part of an attempt, breath-taking in its extent, to account for the coexistence of evil and an all-powerful, all-good God. The gnostics' answer to this difficulty is elaborated in a mythical explanation of the origin of all things from the divine principle, of the occasion of evil, and of its eventual destruction. While the myth often employs language and images which may strike us as bizarre, it addressed and sought to solve genuine problems which also engaged the interest of contemporary philosophers. The chief of these problems was to explain not only how God caused a universe containing suffering and evil to come into existence, but how he managed to cause anything at all. One of the leading ideas of the gnostics about God, an idea they shared with contemporary Middle Platonist philosophers, and with the whole of the subsequent orthodox Christian tradition, was that God cannot change. But if God creates anything, does he not change from being a non-creator to being a creator? The gnostic myth answered this by proposing that there is a multiplicity of ways of being, or dispositions, within God. These dispositions they called Aeons, and while the language of the myth often suggests that we should look upon them as separate, individual beings, we should recall that together they make up the fullness of divinity—the divine Pleroma, as the gnostics called it.

The absolute and transcendent divine principle is called 'Depth' (Bythos), who is made the subject of all the negative attributes which Middle Platonist philosophers predicated of God.[7] He is invisible, unoriginated, beyond the grasp of understanding and of language, existing unchanging from endless ages, and so on. The first of his dispositions, also known as his consort, has three names: 'Purposive Thought' (Ennoia), 'Silence' (Sige) and 'Grace' (Charis). It is here that the gnostic myth tackles the question of the changeability of God. God was always disposed to be actively creative (he always had Purposive Thought), even when he was not actively creative (Silence). He does not change when Silence becomes active in

Purposive Thought, but when this happens it does not happen outside his control, hence Silence, or Purposive Thought, is also called Grace.

Depth and Purposive Thought together produced two 'projections' or Aeons, 'Mind' (Nous) and 'Truth' (Aletheia).[8] Bythos and Nous are masculine in Greek, while Ennoia and Aletheia are feminine. The gnostic myth employs sexual imagery to account for the way Bythos and Ennoia 'produced' Nous and Aletheia. Nous and Aletheia in their turn produced two pairs of Aeons: 'Word' and 'Life' (Logos and Zoe) and 'Man' and 'Church' (Anthropos and Ecclesia). Each pair produced a further pair which produced a further pair until the 'Fullness' (Pleroma) of 30 paired male and female Aeons was achieved. The sexual imagery and the word 'projection' (*probolē*) were meant to suggest that each pair of Aeons came out of the pair which preceded it, and thus was of the same substance. Nevertheless, there was a descending hierarchy in this chain of being. Only Nous, who was produced immediately from Bythos and Ennoia, was capable of comprehending the greatness of the 'Father' (i.e. Bythos). As Bythos himself was utterly transcendent he could not properly be called the cause or father of the Pleroma. These titles were given to Nous, while Bythos was called 'Before-Cause' and 'Before-Father'. At the other end of the hierarchy of divine being was Sophia, 'Wisdom'.

The origin of the material world, and of evil, was accounted for by instability within the divine Pleroma. This was, in fact, a daring theological position. 'God', in a general sense, was seen to be the cause of everything, even matter and evil. The theological difficulties this gave rise to were overcome by the differentiation of aspects within God, so that, while 'God' remained the cause of all, matter and evil could be said not to have been caused directly by God, and especially not by God in his most transcendent aspect. Nevertheless, instability within the Pleroma occurred remarkably high up in the hierarchy: in effect, with Nous himself. For Nous determined to communicate to the other Aeons what he alone was able to comprehend—the greatness of the Father (AH I.2.1). Although this intention was swiftly thwarted by Silence, at the will of the Father, Nous did succeed in introducing into the other Aeons a moderate, though unfulfillable, desire to contemplate Bythos. Sophia, however, the last of the Aeons, was not content with this moderate desire for the unattainable: she rebelled against the harmony and order of the Pleroma, rejected the embrace of her own consort (Theletos, 'The Desired') and violently sought to

16

comprehend the greatness of the Father. The unfulfillable desire (*pothos*) of knowing the Father which Nous had introduced into the other Aeons of the Pleroma became, in the case of Wisdom, a passion, suffering, and disease (*pathos*) (AH I.2.2). Her love and desire for the unattainable was so great, it reduced her to so great a distress, that she was in danger of disintegrating. The measures taken by the other Aeons to prevent this ultimately gave rise to the existence of a world outside the Pleroma.

Matter, evil, and suffering belong to the world beyond the Pleroma which came into being by accident, as it were, but still by the agency of divine Aeons. A 'Limit' (Horos) was set up to contain the divine Pleroma. Sophia was established within the Limit, but her 'Desire' for the Father and her 'Passion' were separated from her and cast out of the Pleroma, beyond the Limit. This separated Desire, now called Achamoth, was itself a spiritual substance, but without shape or form. 'Christ', an Aeon produced along with 'Holy Spirit' by Mind and Truth in order to prevent further instability within the Pleroma, took pity on Achamoth and gave her substantial form. Achamoth was scarcely better off for this attention, however, because she now had an unfulfillable yearning ('Conversion') for the divine realm to which 'Christ' and 'Holy Spirit' had returned. 'Jesus Saviour', who had been produced by all the Aeons together in celebration of the restoration of calm within the Pleroma, then descended and gave Achamoth formation in knowledge (AH I.2.6; 4.5). At the sight of the angels attending the Saviour, Achamoth conceived and gave birth to spiritual substances, which were of the same nature as herself. From the substance of her Conversion towards the Pleroma she formed 'psychic' substances, the first of these being the Demiurge, the creator of the material world — the God of the Old Testament who is worshipped by the ignorant as the only God.[9] This Demiurge formed the material world out of the substance of Achamoth's Passion. Hence it was by nature evil, corruptible and full of sorrows. It is from this matter that the Demiurge created material human beings ('hylics') into some of whom he breathed his own substance, soul, so that they became ensouled human beings ('psychics'). Without his knowledge, however, Achamoth contrived to insinuate some of her spiritual substance into some of the human creatures of the Demiurge and these were the 'pneumatics', the spiritual ones, the gnostics themselves.

It is easy to laugh at the gnostic system, and Irenaeus does.[10] But we should not let the bizarre language of its myths conceal from us the grandeur of this religious system. It sought to take account of all aspects of the human condition: of suffering and sorrow, of the distress and alienation experienced in social, familial and sexual relationships, of the joy and pain of mystical experience, of the achievements and disappointments of intellectual endeavour. It sought to explain all these things in terms of a cosmic drama long since finished. All the distress we suffer is simply part of the cosmic rubbish left behind by the primordial near-catastrophe within the divine realm. The true gnostic knows this, and knows that he or she does not belong to this shadowy world of matter and soul, multiplicity and diversity, but to the divine Pleroma of light and spirit, where universal harmony and unity have long since been restored. The function of the historical Jesus in this scheme was that of revealer of these truths. The revelation was contained in the writings handed on by his disciples. But since this revelation was intended only for the spiritual, by whom alone it could be understood, it was often hidden under allegory or in a numerical code. As the psychics could not penetrate to the spiritual meaning, some of the revelations made to the disciples by Jesus were kept secret from them.

MARCION

Marcion is accorded a place by Irenaeus in his genealogy of gnostic heresies, and he is sometimes treated as a gnostic by modern authors, but the similarities between Marcion's teaching and those of the gnostics are superficial and the differences fundamental (AH I.27.2). Marcion shared with the gnostics the belief that the phenomenal world was created by a lesser God, whose activities are chronicled in the Old Testament. He did not, however, share the gnostic concern for an all-embracing account of the origin and condition of the cosmos. He seems to have been concerned not with the elaboration of myths of cosmogony but with the radically consistent interpretation of the writings which the Christian Church called its Scriptures.

When Marcion was at work, at Rome, in the middle years of the second century, the Christian Scriptures were still, pre-eminently, the books of the Old Testament in the Greek translation known as the Septuagint. The canon of the New Testament achieved its final form only after Marcion, and partly in reaction to him. Nevertheless, there was a body of writings, including gospels and collections of letters by Paul and others, which Christians treated preferentially. Marcion argued that the Christian community could not go on according the status of divine revelation to all this material indiscriminately, because it was inconsistent with itself. In particular, there appeared to be a complete contradiction between the God of the Old Testament and the God whom Jesus called Father. The Old Testament showed the Creator of the world to be vengeful, war-loving, infirm of purpose, and preoccupied with the justice due to him. The God whom Jesus called his Father was a God of love and mercy. Therefore, the Father revealed by Jesus could not be the God of the Old Testament. Marcion found proof of this in a saying of Jesus which survives in Matthew 11:27 and Luke 10:22, but which Marcion probably knew in the form: 'No one knew the Father except the Son, nor the Son except the Father and him to whom the Son chose to reveal (him)' (AH IV.6.1). The Father, then, was not known before he was revealed by Jesus. As the God of the Old Testament had been known before Jesus he could not be the Father of Jesus. In agreement with this insight Marcion rejected the whole of the Old Testament, not as false, but as telling of a God from whom Jesus had come to rescue us. As the material world is the creation of the Old Testament God it is from the material world too that Jesus rescues us, or at least those of us who, like the 'sinners' of the Old Testament, are prepared to reject the sovereignty of the creator God.

Jesus' revelation of a hitherto unknown God was so revolutionary that many, including his own disciples, failed to understand it. The only one who did understand it fully was Paul. His letters, then, form the core of the genuine Christian Scriptures, but they need to be read with care, for the non-comprehending disciples of Jesus and their followers had contaminated them with contradictory references to the Old Testament God and his works. Some of the letters supposed to be of Paul (i.e. the Pastorals) were in fact forgeries, and were to be rejected altogether. The genuine letters all needed to be re-edited. Along with this emended text of Paul, called the Apostolicon, Marcion recognized one Gospel, a severely revised edition of Luke, the evangelist associated with the apostolic endeavours of Paul (AH I.27.4; III.12.12).

OTHER HERESIES

Gnosticism and Marcionism were the most important of the heresies opposed by Irenaeus, but they were not the only ones. Some of the others may not have posed a particular challenge to the communities for whom Irenaeus was concerned, and they do not necessarily merit their place in his taxonomy of gnostic heresy. A number of theological views were current which bore some resemblance to one or another of the doctrines of the gnostics and Marcion, but which were held by Christians who had no other connection with these heresies.

Docetism was the belief that Christ only *appeared* to have been a human being, and to have had a human body, and to have been born of Mary, and to have died on the cross. This view was congenial to many gnostics and to Marcion, but it was by no means unique to them.[11]

Ebionites, on the other hand, were Jewish Christians who rejected the claim that Mary conceived of the Holy Spirit and held that Jesus was the son of Mary and Joseph. Their name derives from the Hebrew for 'poor ones'. According to Irenaeus, they used only the Gospel of Matthew (AH I.26.2; III.11.7). They have nothing in common with gnosticism or Marcionism, and probably owe their place in *Adversus Haereses* to the fact that their denial of the divinity of Jesus seemed to balance the denial by others of his humanity (AH IV.33.4; V.1.3).

Encratites were groups of Christians who practised severe, even extreme, forms of asceticism. The name refers to the self-control which was the goal of their asceticism. Their disdain for the body and its functions seemed to align them with the Marcionites and some of the gnostic schools (AH I.28.1).

Irenaeus' readers would have recognized these names as referring to doctrines not favoured by the mainstream Church. But even within the Great Church there were Christians who, without endorsing the extreme views of the Encratites, had an understanding of salvation which was primarily spiritual, concerned with the soul or the mind, and disregarded the traditional doctrine of the resurrection of the body. Irenaeus defended his belief that the human body is the focus of salvation history against these orthodox Christians, as well as against the heretics who denied the body's redemption and reviled it as the despicable work of a lesser god (AH V.31.1).

Irenaeus likens the proliferation of gnostic doctrines to the mythical Hydra of Lerna slain by Hercules: a monster of many heads, which would sprout more heads from the place where one was cut off.[12] Most of Book II is given over to a refutation, under broad headings, of the whole Valentinian system, and towards the end of the book Irenaeus says that this refutation of the Valentinians can stand as a refutation of all the other heresies (AH II.praef.2; 31.1). He proceeds to offer a few examples, but the book then trails away into a ragbag of arguments against various opinions not directly related to the Valentinian school. When planning his own response to the heretics, the diversity and apparent interrelatedness of their views clearly presented Irenaeus with a problem of organization. He returns to this theme at the beginning of Book III, where he says his opponents are like slippery serpents, trying to slither away in all directions (AH III.2.3). If he were to continue with the detailed refutation of Book II, focused on the specific doctrines of particular schools, the remainder of the work would be tedious, repetitive and immensely long.

Irenaeus overcame this difficulty by choosing one doctrine that most of the major heresies he opposed did have in common: the complete disjunction between the creator God of the Old Testament and the God revealed by Jesus: 'whatever I have said about the Creator to prove that he alone is the God and Father of all, and whatever I shall say in the subsequent books, I say against all the heretics' (AH II.31.1). He thus was able to give unity to his attack upon the diverse schools of thought he had surveyed in Book I by emphasizing one superficial resemblance. Marcion and the gnostics had entirely different reasons for denying that the created order was the work of the one and only God. Nevertheless, they did deny it, and the distinction they drew between the creator God of the Old Testament and the God revealed by Jesus provoked the controlling ideas of the theology which Irenaeus elaborated against all the heresies he opposed. There is only one God, only one creation, and only one purpose of God in creating it and saving it. The one God would reveal himself in the creature he had fashioned from mud, just as he had intended when he first created it, and bestow his own glory upon it.[13] All this is to be seen in the Scriptures, if only they are understood as they were meant to be understood: all this is proclaimed by the Church which preserves and passes on the preaching handed down from the Apostles.

Notes

1   Origen, *De Principiis* I.praef.; IV.2.

2   Cf. *The Nag Hammadi Library in English*, translated by members of the Coptic Gnostic Library Project of the Institute for Antiquity and Christianity, James M. Robinson, Director (San Francisco, 1977).

3 AH I.29.1 – 30.1. Irenaeus had earlier said that some of the followers
   of Carpocrates called themselves 'gnostics' (AH I.25.6).

4 AH I.29.1; cf. I.11.1.

5 AH I.23.2. Irenaeus may have derived this notion from the now lost
   Treatise Against All Heresies of Justin Martyr. The idea was to become
   a commonplace of heresiological literature. It mirrored the claim of
   the orthodox that right belief had been handed down in an unbroken
   tradition stretching back to the Apostles and thus to Jesus.

6 AH I.6.4; 7.1; 7.5.

7 This summary is drawn from Irenaeus' account at AH I.1.1ff.

8 The Greek word *probolē* means something produced, thrown forward
   or outward. *Aiōn* means an age or an eternity, but here it is a technical
   term denominating the 'projections'.

9 *Dēmiourgos* is a Greek word meaning skilled craftsman. It had been
   used by philosophers to describe the Creator, and was taken over by
   the gnostics and used in a disparaging sense to describe the lowly being
   who created the world. Orthodox Christians, Irenaeus among them,
   continued to use it to describe God as the Creator (AH V.17.1).

10 See, for example, AH I.11.4: 'There is nothing to prevent anyone else
   from making up such names, for example: there exists a certain royal
   "Before-Principle", "Before-Unintelligible", "Before-Unsubstantial",
   a "Before-Before-Cylindrical Power" which I name "Gourd". Together
   with the "Gourd" there exists a Power which I call "Utter Emptiness".
   This "Gourd" and "Utter Emptiness", being one, emitted, and yet did
   not emit, a fruit, altogether visible, edible and delicious. This fruit is
   known to language as "Cucumber". With this "Cucumber" there exists
   a Power of the same substance as it, which I call "Melon". These
   Powers, "Gourd", "Utter Emptiness", "Cucumber" and "Melon", have
   emitted the remaining multitude of the delirious melons of the Valentinians.' The word translated here by 'melon' could be used in Greek as
   a term of personal endearment. But it refers to a kind of gourd which
   was not eaten until it had been turned quite ripe by the sun.

11 AH I.24.4; IV.33.5; V.1.2.

12 AH I.30.15. At AH II.31.3 Irenaeus says the heretics are the precursors
   of the seven-headed dragon foretold in Revelation 12.

13 The term 'earth creature' will appear frequently in these pages. Some
   Old Testament scholars have suggested that this term be used instead
   of 'Adam' when discussing the theology of the first chapters of Genesis.
   See Phyllis Trible, *God and the Rhetoric of Sexuality* (Philadelphia,
   1978), p. 140. For reasons I shall give later, it is also particularly useful
   when discussing the theology of Irenaeus.

3

The one God

INTRODUCTION

Orthodox Christians believe that God is Father, Son and Holy Spirit and that Father, Son and Holy Spirit are not three different names for the same thing. One might be forgiven for supposing that orthodox Christians would not also want to say that God is one. But they do; and the difficulty of saying that God is three and God is one without abandoning the expectation of being taken seriously accounts for much of the history of Christian theology. The doctrines of the oneness of God and of the divine Trinity have become so much part of the same problem that it is difficult to think of the one without the other. As Irenaeus has much to say about the oneness of God and about the divine Trinity, and as he wrote at such an early stage in the development of Christian doctrine, it is tempting to ask how he dealt with this intriguing problem. The answer may be disappointing. It does not seem to have worried him much at all. For Irenaeus, the statements that God is one and that God is Father, Son and Holy Spirit were answers to different questions. He does not seem to have been too much troubled by the problems that arise when the two statements are brought together as an answer to one question about the nature of God. If we bear this in mind our investigation of Irenaeus' doctrine of God will be made, at least initially, less complicated.

Christian apologists writing before Irenaeus insisted on the oneness of God against the claims of pagan polytheism. Later theologians had to reconcile this traditional doctrine with belief in

23

the divine Trinity. Irenaeus' preoccupation with the doctrine that God is one was occasioned and shaped not by opposition to pagan polytheism or by the difficulties occasioned by Christian belief in the divine Trinity, but by opposition to the views of his Christian opponents concerning the Creator of the world. For our purposes we may distinguish two approaches to God against which Irenaeus wrote. The simpler of these is the view that there are two gods, vying for the allegiance of humankind and having nothing to do with one another. This is the underlying thesis of Marcionism. The lesser God is the creator of the material and psychic world, over which he rules. The greater God is purely spiritual. He has no interest in or dealings with the lesser God or his creation. He redeems his own from this creation and bears them off to his own realm.

Marcion postulated two contrasting gods in order to account for an irreconcilable opposition between the God of the Old Testament and the God of Jesus, and between the material realm of the former and the spiritual realm of the latter. While a contrast between the spiritual and the material was also very important for the gnostics, they had more sophisticated reasons for acknowledging multiplicity in God, reflecting, in part, the theological speculations of contemporary Middle Platonist philosophers. When such philosophers postulated more than one God they did not suppose these Gods to be in opposition. On the contrary, it was central to their conception that they should be in harmony. There must be more than one God, it was argued, because the things one wants to say about God are mutually incompatible. On the one hand, God must be utterly transcendent, unchanging, incorporeal, invisible, beyond the grasp and description of created intellect, and so on. But, as God is also thought of as the provident, benign creator and ruler of all that is good, the question arises: how is God to reveal and achieve his benevolent, saving purposes when his transcendence makes it impossible for him to communicate with anything beyond himself? The solution to this problem was to suggest that a subordinate god (or gods) effects the saving will of the first God for his creation. The same concept is also to be found in orthodox Christian theologians, like Justin Martyr, and became very significant for the development of the orthodox doctrine of the Trinity. There are traces of it even in Irenaeus. The gnostics' theory of a multiplicity of Aeons, each representing a different divine attribute or disposition, is an exaggerated development of the same idea.

It was the claim of the gnostics and Marcion that the creator of the world we live in is not the only, or even the highest, God that, more than any other issue, preoccupied the attention of Irenaeus and dominated his major work. The identity of God with the Creator of the world is, he says, the first and greatest of the subjects which he must dispute with the heretics (AH II.1.1). He seems never willing to let pass an opportunity to refute the heretics on this, no matter how thoroughly he has argued his case previously, and it seems to have been here that the heretics most severely abraded his own religious sensitivity, not simply towards God, but towards the world he believed to be the work of God. His religious awe of and love for the Creator God went hand in hand with a religious awe of and love for the world he believed that God to have created. The whole force of his argument is turned toward proving that the creator God whom the heretics deride is the only God there is: that he alone is all-powerful, all-good, all-knowing, all-loving. Irenaeus' own piety is so intimately caught up in this battle that his argument is sometimes weakened in consequence. He often expresses his amazement that anyone should suppose that a weak, foolish, jealous God, or anything less than God could have brought into being so rich and manifold a world.[1] In this he seems oblivious of the fact that disgust at the phenomenal world lies close to the heart of the thesis of the heretics that it cannot have been created by the best and highest God. He argues, for example, that to say that angels created our world independently of God is to imply that angels are more powerful than God, since they would have achieved a great thing, while God would not (AH II.2.1).

Although Irenaeus takes up some of his opponents' arguments about the existence of evil in the created world, he does not really come to grips with their generally negative assessment of created reality; principally, I suggest, because he is incapable of achieving any kind of imaginative, sympathetic insight into a world-view in which the phenomenal world is negatively assessed. He takes it as given that the created world, in all its rich diversity, is a place of wonder and delight, and deduces that it has been created by a God of infinitely rich diversity and goodness whose purpose is that his sentient and intelligent creatures should endure for ever, always discovering new occasions for wonder and delight in God. 'The love which is in God', he says, 'is rich and unenvious and more bounteous than anyone might require.'[2] And 'when the form of this world has passed away, and humankind has been renewed, and has so far advanced toward its maturity in incorruption that it can grow old no longer, then there shall be a new heaven and a new earth in which humankind will remain always new, ever talking of new things with

God' (AH V.36.1). Conversely, he seems to suppose that the heretics' disgust for the creation is due simply to their mistaken belief that it has been created by a despicable and lesser God.

The arguments Irenaeus advances in Book II sometimes appear condensed, and it is not always obvious which heretical theory is under attack. He seems to have thought that an argument against the doctrine of God in the Valentinian school would work against Marcion's doctrine of God as well (AH II.1.2, 4). However, he knew well enough that there are some very significant differences between Marcion and the Valentinians on the doctrine of God. Marcion, for example, did not concern himself with the question of where the God who created this world came from or how he was related to the God of love revealed by Jesus Christ. He simply insisted that there was absolutely no relationship between the two: rather there existed a vast, impassable gulf between them. For the Valentinians, on the other hand, the supreme deity and the creator of the world, although vastly separated from one another, belong in the same chain of being. We need not suppose that they were being disingenuous when they said, as Irenaeus knew they said, that there was but one God.[3] Indeed, it may be doubted that the Valentinians would even have approved of the description of the Demiurge as 'god'. Irenaeus himself seems to have had considerable trouble nailing down exactly what the word 'god' means in the Valentinian system: sometimes he suggests that the whole Pleroma is 'God', containing the supreme God within it.[4]

ONE GOD

One of Irenaeus' favourite rhetorical tools is the dilemma: he tries to force his opponents to a position where they must accept either of two equally unacceptable alternatives. This is a form of rhetorical argument especially open to abuse, because it is often an easy matter to suggest that a choice must be made between two alternatives when, in fact, other possibilities may exist. The modern reader is likely to be irritated when Irenaeus is discovered vigorously demolishing points of view never held by his opponents but postulated by Irenaeus himself as the horns of a dilemma, on which, he says, they are caught. Although Irenaeus was not above rhetorical subterfuge, he did consider the accurate reporting of the views of his opponents, or exposure of their absurdity, as he called it, to be one of his most effective weapons against them.[5] It should not be too readily supposed that he resorts to cheap misrepresentations of his opponents' views in order to score rhetorical victories. When he does present a distorted picture of his opponents' positions this owes much to his own inability or refusal to achieve any kind of sympathetic insight into their religious outlook. No stranger to allegory or symbolic language in his own exegesis and theological elaboration, he often seems quite unable to grant that the symbolic language employed by his opponents has its own grammar, different from that of logical or narrative discourse. He thinks it a triumph to show that what the Valentinians say in symbolic language looks very foolish when read not as symbolic but as factual narrative or geometric description.

The distorting effect of this blind spot in Irenaeus' perception of his opponents' positions is especially evident in his ridiculing of their description of the things of the phenomenal world as images made in the likeness of the 'real' world above, or as shadows of that world. He says, for example, that things in our world cannot be images of the 'real' world because they are ephemeral and thus do no honour to the 'real' world, which is eternal; that if things in our world are shadows of things above then the so-called 'spiritual' world above must in fact be both corporeal and transient, since only bodies cast shadows, and, as the shadows are transient, so must the bodies be that cast them (AH II.7.1; 8.1). Again, he argues that if one thing is an image of another then *all* the properties of the image must be reflections of similar properties in that of which it is the image (AH II.7.2–6). If this were true, any attempt to use language symbolically would be open to mockery. For, by this argument, the Singer of the Song of Songs could not compare her beloved to a gazelle or a young stag unless he had four legs, hooves, antlers, and so on. Irenaeus seems to have been aware of the weakness of this kind of argument, aware that his opponents will object that they did not expect their symbolic language to be understood in so crassly a literal sense (AH II.8.2), but, rather truculently, he refuses to yield:

> if they say that they are images of the 'Projection', not according to figure nor according to form, but according to number and order, we reply, in the first instance, that these should not be said to be images and likenesses of those Aeons which are above: for if they have neither their shape nor their figure, how can they be their images? (AH II.7.7)

This attempt to wrong-foot his opponents by reading as literal what they meant as symbolic characterizes the argument of Book II from the outset. The assault on the heretical doctrine of God begins with a series of arguments which press geometry into the service of theology. Irenaeus knows that his opponents did not mean what they said about God to be understood in terms analogous to geometry, for he offers advice on what to say when they counter-claim that what he is attacking is not their doctrine of God at all (AH II.4.2; 5.2). Nevertheless, he presents these geometric arguments first, perhaps because he thought they would be more readily accessible to his readers. He begins by drawing upon a definition of God with roots deep in the Greek philosophical tradition: 'God encloses all things immeasurably and is himself enclosed by nothing'.[6] This formula had already been employed by Philo and the Valentinians and is echoed, in words which Irenaeus will quote, in *The Shepherd of Hermas*, a Christian work of the early second century.[7] Irenaeus brings this definition to bear upon the debate by exploiting the Valentinian use of the word 'Pleroma'. For the Valentinians, this had become a technical term to indicate that the original production of spiritual reality reached its completion and perfection with the projection of the thirtieth Aeon. The 30 Aeons make up the Pleroma, the 'Fullness'. All Christians would have been familiar and comfortable with talk of the divine Pleroma in a less specific sense, indicating simply the fullness or perfection of God, as for example in Colossians 1:19: 'For in him all the fullness of God was pleased to dwell' (cf. Col 2:9). Drawing upon this background, Irenaeus speaks of God as 'the fullness of all', which he supposes to be another way of saying that God alone contains everything and is himself contained by nothing. Naturally, Irenaeus believes that this description fits only the creator God, above whom there can therefore be no other Pleroma and besides whom there can be no other God. For, if there is anything above him or apart from him he will not be the fullness of all, he will not be the one who contains without being himself contained.

An important, but unstated, assumption behind these 'geometrical' arguments is that there does not exist a void or vacuum.[8] Granted that no void exists, if there is something external to God which he does not contain, he must be contained by it, and limited by it. But, Irenaeus says, the Valentinians do acknowledge something outside the Pleroma, for they say that Sophia's 'Desire' was separated from her and cast outside (AH II.1.3). However, whatever is outside the Pleroma must either surround it on all sides, and thus be greater than it, or be at a distance from it. If it is at a distance from the Pleroma, there must be some third reality which separates the Pleroma from what is outside it. This third reality will be partly contiguous with the Pleroma and partly contiguous with what is outside it. Each of these three realities will limit, or define, one another where they touch. But if they are defined on one side, they will need to be defined on all their other sides as well. We must therefore postulate other realities to define them on their other sides, and these will require further realities to define them on *their* other sides, and so on. It follows that if one allows the existence of any one reality which is not contained by God one will have to grant either that that reality is greater than God, completely containing him, or else that there is an infinity of finite realities outside of God.

Irenaeus was clearly impressed by the rhetorical value of showing that an argument for the existence of something outside of God could lead to the unwelcome consequence of an infinite number of realities on a par with 'god', and he argues in similar fashion against Marcion's claim that the two gods are separated by an immense gulf (AH II.1.4). Assuming once more that what separates the two cannot be a void, Irenaeus says there must be some third reality between them. Again, and presumably for the same reasons, he says one will not be able to stop at three. By postulating two gods Marcion has obliged himself to admit an infinity of gods. Nor will there be any way of telling what, in this jumble, are the relative positions of our world and the 'higher realities' postulated by the heretics.

Even if there were such a profusion of gods, each of them should be content with his own realm and not busy himself invading the realms of other gods in the way that the divine beings of the Valentinians and Marcion's god of love invade the realm of the God who created us and our world. For gods who behave thus show themselves to be unjust and envious and thus not what a god should be. Nor should a god whose power extends over only a tiny part of an infinite whole be called the All-powerful. Yet to deny God this title is to blaspheme him (AH II.1.5).

The alternative to this endless multiplication of gods is to admit that there is only one God, who freely created everything that is, who contains all things without being limited or defined by the things he contains.

After these arguments against there being some other reality outside of God Irenaeus turns to the claims made by the Valentinians about the creator of the phenomenal world. He acknowledges that they wish to locate the Demiurge within the chain of being which has its origin with the highest God, but argues that no logical purpose is served by postulating the existence of such a chain of being (AH II.2.3). The only reason for suggesting that such a chain of being exists is to establish some kind of distance between the highest God and the creator of the material world, and the reason for hypothesizing such a distance must be that it was either not possible for the highest God to create such a world directly, or else not worthy of him. But if it was not possible for God to have created the world directly then he is shown not to be all-powerful, but to have been in need of the assistance of lesser beings who acted as his agents. If it was not worthy of the highest God to create such a world directly, then neither was it worthy of him to create it indirectly, for he is just as much responsible for it if he created it by the use of secondary agents and instruments as if he created it directly and immediately (AH II.2.4). Nor will it do to suppose that lesser agents created the world without the knowledge or permission of the supreme God, for this would imply that he is either ignorant of what lesser agents do, or uninterested in what they do, or improvident respecting it (AH II.2.1–2; 3.1). If, however, God is to satisfy the definition of God, if he is all-knowing, all-provident, and all-powerful, then he could not allow secondary beings to bring into existence a creation in respect of which he remained ignorant, indifferent, improvident or powerless. So as the world we inhabit does exist, it must exist by the will and the power of the highest God, just as that God intended it should exist, whether he created it with or without the mediation of agents and instruments. Since the only reason for saying that he created it through the mediation of agents is to absolve him of responsibility for the world as it is, one might as well allow that God created it directly.[9]

The Valentinian chain of being fails to achieve what is claimed for it in another respect also. Fundamental to the concept of the chain of being is the idea of a lessening or diminishing of whatever is communicated from one Aeon in the chain to the next. Thus, only the Aeon projected directly from Bythos is capable of knowing him. The further one descends the chain of being, the more remote one becomes from the principle of all, the more likely it becomes that some kind of misadventure should befall, such as is said to have befallen Sophia. But, says Irenaeus, if each succeeding Aeon is said to be projected from the being of the one preceding it, then it should have the same substance as the one preceding it. Hence, there will be no diminution of being in consequence of a lowly place in the hierarchy of being. Sophia should communicate in the being of

Bythos and comprehend him just as much as Nous does (AH II.4.1). If the relationship between Sophia and her yoke-fellow, Theletos, is easily broken, then the link binding each of the other pairs of Aeons must be equally fragile (AH II.12.3-4).

Although it might seem that Irenaeus is here, once again, unfairly forcing the imagery employed by the Valentinians, I believe he has discovered a major weakness in their case. For all their disparagement of the material world and its creator, the gnostics never drew an absolute distinction between the material and the spiritual realms. It was important to them to have a unitary solution of the problem of why the world is as it is. They could never be happy, as the Marcionites were, and later the Manichees would be, with two primordial and irreducible principles. Somehow or other, all of reality, evil and pain as well as beauty and happiness, must be ultimately reducible to a single cause. The Valentinian system was meant to show that absolutely everything, including evil and suffering, derives ultimately from a single principle. This is a courageous and honest attempt to solve the problem of evil. But the Valentinians receive no credit for it from Irenaeus, whose assault upon it is devastating. The gnostics admit, he says, that there is ultimately only one divine principle, they admit that there is suffering within the Godhead itself (AH II.16.3; 17.8). For all their multiplication of intermediary beings and events between the highest God and human misery, it remains the case, as Irenaeus triumphantly proclaims, that the gnostics' 'Father' is the cause of all the evil their system is designed to explain and liberate them from (AH II.17.10). What is the point of an elaborate ramification of intermediary beings if, at the end of the day, one has to admit that there is only one ultimate principle of all that is? (AH II.16.2-3). If one God explains everything, why invent more?

The more complicated an explanation is, the easier it is to fault. The Valentinians would say that the complexity of their solution simply reflects the complexity of reality. But Irenaeus, who is under no obligation to explain everything, since he admits he does not know everything (AH II.28.1-2), is able to show that the complicated solution of the Valentinians counts both too many Aeons, and too few (AH II.12.8). It claims that there is a Pleroma of 30 Aeons, but Bythos, who is without origin, who is not projected from another, who is beyond comprehension and without form, ought not to be numbered with the 29 Aeons who are originated, projected, have form, and may be comprehended (AH II.12.1). On the other hand, it seems that 30 is too small a tally of Aeons, for there is no reason why Limit, and Christ, and Holy Spirit, and Saviour should not be numbered among them, for, like the Aeons, they are projected from the Only-Begotten (AH II.12.7).

The Valentinians, Irenaeus mordantly observes, claim that God is totally unknowable, and then set about describing him in great detail, fracturing him into different, subordinated dispositions, often based on human psychology (AH II.13.3). Not only is it crass anthropomorphism to attempt to explain the indescribable God in this way, it is quite unnecessary. For God is entirely simple; that is to say, without composition; he has no parts, his acts cannot be distinguished and classified. When we contemplate a human act we can distinguish between the conception of a plan of action, its thinking through, the intention to effect it, the will to effect it, and the actual doing of it. But no such distinctions can be discovered in the acts of God. For God, thinking, planning, willing, and executing his will are all the one act, all achieved simultaneously.[10]

GOD AND HIS CREATION

Profound as was the gnostics' sense of the transcendence of God, Irenaeus' was deeper still. For the gnostics, the transcendence of God over this world is ultimately relative: a matter of distance. For Irenaeus it is absolute. The gnostics understood all reality to be a continuous whole. Despite the vast distance between them, God and matter stand in the same continuum, the same chain of being. Indeed, it is part of the purpose of the notion of the chain of being to account both for the distance between God and matter and for their connection with one another. Just as light from the sun falls more weakly on the surface of the planet Jupiter than it does on the earth, so, in the Valentinian scheme, the further removed anything in the continuum of being is from the source of being the weaker will be its hold on being. It is because of this sense of the unity of being that the gnostics can conceive of the possibility that particles which belong much closer to the source might be forced by some catastrophe into the outer reaches of the continuum and yet be able to travel back to their proper place. The alienation which is such a marked feature of the Valentinian world-view was relative. One might suffer a terrifying sense of dislocation, of being far removed from the source of one's being and from one's proper place in relation to that source, but there was some comfort to be had in the thought that, wherever one was, one was in the same continuum of being as everything else, including the source of being. Even more comforting was the hope of reversing the outward movement, of turning back to the centre and source of one's existence.

Irenaeus completely rejects this concept of the continuity of all reality, and this is one of his most profound points of disagreement with the gnostics. It may also be one of his most significant contributions to the subsequent orthodox theological tradition.[11] For Irenaeus, there is absolutely no continuity of being between God and creation. He sweeps aside the gnostic description of the universe, with all its complexity, by denying that there is a chain of being, denying that there is any kind of substantial continuity between God and his creation. God and our world do not belong to the same continuum: there is nothing linking our world to its creator. Creation does not share in the same substance as God, in however attenuated and sullied a form. Rather, God is the only reality, the only thing that really *is*, and over against God, called into existence out of nothingness by God, and held in being, poised over nothingness by God, is everything that God creates. There is no substance or essence or being common to all created things, much less common to created things and God. The only 'substance' of created things, all that underpins them, is the will of God. The gnostics, he says, 'think they can account for the origin of the substance of matter, while refusing to believe that God has bestowed existence on all created things, just as he willed, employing his own power and will in the place of substance'.[12] Paradoxically, just because God's transcendence over creation is absolute, he is immediately present to his creation in a way impossible within the Valentinian scheme. In Irenaeus' view, the being which in the Valentinian scheme pulses out from Bythos to engender the Fullness is confined entirely to God himself. Only God *exists*, only God *is*. Everything else 'exists' not in virtue of a sharing in the being which is God, but because God creates it, calls it into existence out of nothingness, bestows upon it its creaturely existence. All existing things, instead of occupying different grades in a hierarchy or chain of being, are immediately present to the God who creates them, or, as Irenaeus likes to say, they are in his hands.[13]

To express this profound difference between God and his creation, and despite his low opinion of Greek philosophy (AH II.14.2–4; 27.1), Irenaeus draws upon the Platonic distinction between Being and Becoming, a formula which had become commonplace in the popular philosophical schools of the day and which was destined to exercise a major influence on the development of several Christian doctrines. Irenaeus used this formula to assert that only God *is* and that everything else is in a state of coming into being or passing out of it, of being generated or corrupted.

The distinction between Being and Becoming is set out in the *Timaeus* thus:

> first then, in my judgement, we must make a distinction and ask, What is that which always is and has no becoming; and what is that which is always becoming and never is? That which is apprehended by intelligence and reason is always in the same state; but that which is conceived by opinion with the help of sensation and without reason, is always in a process of becoming and perishing and never really is.[14]

The concept of the absolute transcendence of God with respect to his creation and the consequent immediacy of his presence to it, which Irenaeus elaborates with the aid of this Platonic distinction, underlies the whole of his theological conception. We shall meet it again and again in the following pages.

Notes

1 Cf. AH II.2.1; 4.3; 10.3; 25.2; 26.3; 29.2; 30.3; III.praef.

2 AH III.praef.; cf. II.10.3; 11.1; III.10.6; 16.7; IV.14.2; 20.11; V.32.1; 33.4.

3 AH I.22.1: 'Almost all the heretics say, indeed, that God is one, but by their evil opinion they distort him . . .'.

4 Cf. Richard Norris, 'The transcendence and freedom of God: Irenaeus, the Greek tradition and gnosticism' in William R. Schoedel and Robert L. Wilken (eds), *Early Christian Literature and the Classical Intellectual Tradition: In Honorem Robert M. Grant* (Théologie historique 54; Paris, 1979), pp. 87–100 (pp. 90–1).

5 AH I.9.1; 31.3; III.praef.; IV.praef.2; V.praef.

6 AH II.1.2; cf. William R. Schoedel, 'Enclosing, not enclosed: The early Christian doctrine of God' in *Early Christian Literature and the Classical Intellectual Tradition*, pp. 75–86. Also of value on Irenaeus' use of this definition of God is Rowan Greer, 'The dog and the mushrooms: Irenaeus's view of the Valentinians assessed' in *The Rediscovery of Gnosticism: Proceedings of the International Conference on Gnosticism at Yale, New Haven, Connecticut, March 28–31, 1978*, I: *The School of Valentinus*, ed. Bentley Layton (Leiden, 1980), pp. 146–75.

7 Philo, *De Somniis* I.63; I.185; *De Migratione Abrahami* 182; 192; Epiphanius, *Panarion* 31.5.3. 'God . . . who contains all things and is himself contained by nothing': *Shepherd of Hermas*, Mandate 1.1; cf. AH II.30.9; IV.20.2.

8 The non-existence of a void or vacuum in nature had been discussed by Aristotle and by Stoic philosophers, and would have been taken for granted by most philosophers contemporary with Irenaeus. The Valentinians had spoken of the expulsion of Achamoth into 'places of shadow and emptiness' (AH I.4.1–2). Irenaeus later argues that if there were such a void either it must have come into existence in the same way as the other Aeons and thus belong inside the Pleroma and not outside it, and be of the same nature as the other Aeons, or else it must be co-eternal with Bythos and of the same nature as him (AH II.4.1).

9 AH II.2.1–4; 3.1–2; 5.3.

10 AH II.2.4; 3.2; 13.3; 28.4–5.

11 Cf. G. May, *Schöpfung aus dem Nichts. Die Entstehung der Lehre von der creatio ex nihilo* (Berlin, 1978), pp. 170–81.

12 AH II.10.2; cf. 10.4 and 30.9: 'by himself alone he freely and voluntarily created and disposed and perfected all things, and his will is the substance of all things'.

13 AH IV.19.2; 20.1; cf. Dem 45. Irenaeus frequently refers to the hand, or hands, of God when speaking of the fashioning of the earth creature: see below, pp. 51, 78.

14 Plato, *Timaeus* 27D–28A (trans. Jowett).

4

Knowing the one God as Father, Son and Holy Spirit

INTRODUCTION

Many of the theological themes which we will be examining in this and subsequent chapters, rich as they might appear to us in their own right, were originally devised to serve as arguments, drawn from Scripture, for the unity of God.

Neither the Valentinians nor Marcion dismissed the Old Testament as an empty fable. Both groups of heretics regarded the Old Testament as an authentic record of the deeds of the creator God. However, as Marcion considered that there was a complete and absolute disjunction between the God of Jesus and the creator God, the Old Testament was of value to him only as a means of pointing up the contrast between the vengeful, war-loving, envious, and just God of the Old Testament and the God of love revealed by Jesus. Even to allow this much validity to the Old Testament left the way open for Irenaeus to argue against Marcion out of the Old Testament. For just as Marcion had sought to show the antithesis between the Old Testament God and the God of Jesus by setting side by side texts from the Old Testament and from his own, modified, New Testament, so Irenaeus undertakes to show a fundamental harmony and continuity between the Old Testament and the New, and thus to demonstrate that there is but one God who is revealed in both. Irenaeus is more constrained in his use of the New Testament against Marcion, because Marcion did not attach any value at all to those parts of it which he excluded from his canon—they represented merely the confusion of thought of most of the disciples of Jesus

36

and their inability to free themselves from the trammels of the Old Testament God. Irenaeus recognizes this restriction, for he promises an assault upon Marcion drawn exclusively from those parts of the New Testament which Marcion did accept (AH I.27.4; III.12.12). No part of *Adversus Haereses* meets such a description, and if Irenaeus ever fulfilled the promise the resulting work has not survived.

With the gnostics, Irenaeus' problem is not that his opponents restrict the amount of Scripture available as a basis for argument, but that they expand it, drawing upon a tradition handed down by the disciples and not fully represented in the New Testament writings but reflected in the large number of pseudepigraphal writings put out by the gnostics themselves, often under the name of one or another of the disciples of Jesus mentioned in the New Testament. Obviously, Irenaeus needed to argue for a means of limiting what is to be regarded as authentic Scripture. In particular, he needed to be able to restrict the number of Gospels associated with the Apostles to the four of the New Testament (AH III.9.1 – 11.9). This still left him with much in common with the Valentinians, for they did not reject as unauthentic any of the books of the Bible which he acknowledged. Rather, they disputed the interpretation of these books, arguing that some reflected the history of the Demiurge who exists far beneath the realm of real divinity, that others used allegory to tell the story of the fall and redemption of Sophia which was spelt out more plainly in their own Scriptures. In particular, the Valentinians and other gnostics made a great deal of allegorical and numerological exegesis of the New Testament, especially of the sayings, parables, and miracles of Jesus.

Irenaeus was thus able to draw much more widely upon his own Bible in argument with the gnostics than with Marcion, and to argue not about the authenticity of these works but about their authentic interpretation.

Modern theologians commonly distinguish between an immanent and an economic theology of the Trinity. An immanent theology of the Trinity attempts some account of the way God is in himself; it asks questions about the eternal relationships between Father, Son, and Spirit and their essential oneness. An economic doctrine of the Trinity concerns itself with the way God reveals himself in and to his creation. It is called an 'economic' doctrine because it has to do with God in relation to his plan for the salvation of humankind, and the word 'economy' was commonly used by Greek-speaking theologians, Irenaeus among them, to refer to this plan of salvation.

Some theologians sometimes give the impression that it is the immanent theology of the Trinity, the working out of the knotty problem of how God can be both three and one, that is more important. But, in fact, the immanent theology of the Trinity should be, and most often has been, subservient to the economic theology of the Trinity. We know that there is a Trinity only because God has revealed himself to us. Most Christians worship God not simply because he is there, but because he has revealed himself to them in love. We need to ponder the intractable questions about the eternal relationships between Father, Son, and Holy Spirit only to the extent that these can help us to understand something of the mystery of the utterly transcendent, invisible, unknowable, unnameable God who reveals himself to us as a God of justice, mercy, and compassion, a God who seeks us out and calls us into his own life, a God who enters the lives of his creatures even to the extent of being brutalized and murdered by them. We need to consider the Trinity in itself only in order to avoid misunderstanding the God of our salvation.

Irenaeus wrote before debates about the proper understanding of the God of our salvation pushed the Trinitarian theology of the Great Church into metaphysics, before the emphasis shifted to the immanent theology of the Trinity. Although there are the beginnings of a metaphysical theology of the Trinity in his writings, he presents us, for the most part, with a highly developed economic theology of the Trinity. He is more concerned with the ways in which Father, Son and Holy Spirit are related to us, rather than with the ways in which they are related to one another. Although this is largely due to his position in a primitive stage of the development of Trinitarian theology, it is also one of the reasons for his continuing popularity. Questions about how God is related to us are much more interesting than questions about how he is related to himself, and not nearly so taxing on the mind. Our investigation of Irenaeus' Trinitarian doctrine will therefore take its starting point from his account of how we come to know God.

KNOWING GOD

Because of his absolute transcendence, God in himself cannot be comprehended or known by human beings. He can, however, be known through his creative providence, and by the power of reason with which he endows us, without any need of special 'revelation' on his part.[1] This is the source of Irenaeus' constant insistence on the greatness and diversity of the world about him. He believes that all of the things he perceives with his senses, in all their extravagant diversity and all their exuberant beauty, owe their existence not to the wash of some tide of being, not to the intervention of angels or spirits, but directly and immediately to the will of God (AH II.10.2–4). Before piety or religion or revelation even enter the discussion, Irenaeus believes that human beings should be aware of the immediacy of the presence to them of the God who absolutely transcends them.

Whereas the gnostics understood salvation in terms of a return from the dark outer reaches of the continuum of being toward the bright centre, Irenaeus sees it in terms of the utterly free, loving, almost capricious, decision of the absolutely transcendent God to lift his creation up to himself: to make his earth creature close to the uncreated (AH IV.38.3). Humankind, without losing its creaturely status (which would, of course, be impossible), is destined to come to share some of the qualities of the uncreated God: most especially the qualities of immortality and incorruptibility. This transformation will be brought about, after a lengthy period of development, when the creature finally sets created eyes on the uncreated God. There is no power of vision within the creature which can, of its own accord, develop to a stage at which it can see God. God will be seen only because he chooses to make himself visible, and this is something God will do gradually, keeping pace with the creature's process of development towards God. Since the power of seeing in question here is not a mystic, inward vision, but ordinary human eyesight, if God is to be visible at all it will be as an object available to human eyesight.[2] In fact, God has chosen to become visible to us as a human being, Jesus of Nazareth.

When Irenaeus read in St John's Gospel that Christ said to Philip 'He who has seen me has seen the Father' (John 14:9; cf. John 12:45: 'he who sees me sees him who sent me'; and John 8:19: 'if you knew me you would know my Father also') he understood this in a perfectly literal sense. The Son is, he says, what is visible of the Father, while the Father is what remains invisible of the Son (AH IV.6.6).

Some scholars have argued that, for Irenaeus, the Son is, from all eternity, 'visible' in a way that the Father is not.[3] Irenaeus' words on this subject do, in fact, have something of a gnostic ring, and it is possible that he may be drawing upon a source, even a gnostic or gnosticizing source, in which the Son is represented as being, in his essential, eternal nature, capable of being seen or comprehended.[4] It is doubtful, however, that Irenaeus shares this rather sophisticated theology. His view is more simple. In himself, God is invisible: he cannot be seen or comprehended or measured in any way because there are no limits to him, no boundaries or surfaces that can be measured or observed by the senses.[5] If this infinite God is to be seen or comprehended, he will need, in some way, to become finite and measurable, because human beings are only able to see and comprehend things of definite shape and limited extent. Doubtless God could tell us about himself by the means of angels and other messengers, but if he is to reveal himself a limit will have to be found to his infinite being and a measure put to his immensity. In Irenaeus' view, the human being, Jesus of Nazareth, is precisely this: God made visible and touchable, God who can speak to human beings and be heard by them, God searching out his own creation and carrying it home on his shoulders (AH V.15.2), God who can be tortured and murdered. On the cross of Jesus, the unseen God who created everything in power, artistry, and wisdom, and who carries it, holds it in being, is seen to be carried, held up, on his own creation (AH V.18.1–2). The divinity of Christ is not hidden by or under his humanity. On the contrary, it is revealed through it, because the humanity limits and defines the divinity, allows it to be measured and comprehended. To see this human being is to see God made visible, to see what can be seen of the Father. This theology is obviously and profoundly influenced by John's Gospel, in which, significantly, there is no account of the transfiguration of Jesus because he manifests his glory precisely in his flesh (John 2:11): his glory as of the only Son of the Father is made visible by his having become flesh, living amongst human beings, and being murdered by them (John 1:14; 12:23).

It cannot be supposed that in becoming limited and measurable God ceases to be infinite and immense, and so Irenaeus says that while the Son is what is visible of the Father, the Father is what is invisible of the Son.[6] Because the Son 'comprehends' the incomprehensible Father, because he has, or rather is, the 'measure' of the immeasurable Father he is able to reveal the Father, to make him known (AH IV.4.2). The Valentinians had said that Mind alone was able to comprehend the immeasurable greatness of the Father, and that he conceived the plan of revealing that greatness to the other Aeons (AH I.2.1). In very similar fashion, Irenaeus says that, while the Father is invisible and without defining characteristics so far as we are concerned, he is known by his own Word and that Word then

40

expresses the inexpressible (AH IV.6.3). It is not just the intellectual comprehension of the Father by the Son that Irenaeus has in view here, but rather the physical shape, the limited form and extension that the Godhead takes on in the human being Jesus. Again, in the Valentinian scheme, Silence prevents Mind from revealing the Father's greatness (AH I.2.1), and Irenaeus also speaks of the Son guarding and administering the Father's invisibility. This is not because the Father must remain forever beyond the gaze of mortals. Rather, since human beings will never completely comprehend God, or know all there is to know of him, they will always be able to advance without limit in the knowledge of him. The Son is the 'steward of the Father's glory': he both gradually reveals the Father to humankind in the measure that they can comprehend, and preserves the Father's invisibility 'lest at any time humankind should become contemptuous of God, and so that there will always be something further to which they can advance'.[7]

The idea that the incarnate Son is God made visible, which is fundamental to Irenaeus' understanding of revelation, also has significant implications for his understanding of human nature, of the person of Christ, and of the divine Trinity. For, if Christ's humanity is not something that sullies or conceals his divinity, but rather makes that divinity available to human perception, then the same is true of the humanity we share with Christ. We need not look upon our humanity as something that comes between us and God, or puts us at a distance from God. On the contrary, precisely in our humanity we can be, and, indeed, are called to be, revealers of divinity, bearers of divine glory, the means by which God is glorified (AH IV.20.7). If Christ is God made visible, the only qualification we need to make about his divinity is to say that it is visible, whereas in the Father the same divinity is invisible.

Post-Nicene orthodox Trinitarian theology subordinates the Son to the Father at least to the extent that it says the Son has his origin in the Father, while the Father is without origin. Although Irenaeus could hardly avoid speaking of the relationship between Father and Son in terms of generation, he does not assign the same significance to this idea as the later tradition does (Dem 43; 47). For him, the divinity of the Son is not of a lesser order: it is simply the infinite, immense divinity of the Father made finite and measureable and therefore visible and comprehensible. A distinction of persons within the Godhead is acknowledged, not because of any insight into the mystery of the divine nature, but because it is believed that in Jesus of Nazareth the God who never ceases to be invisible, to be utterly beyond our apprehension, is made visible and tangible. Hence the visibility of God in Christ is, for Irenaeus, the basis of the Christian belief that there is a Trinity.

When contemporaries of Jesus looked at him what they saw was God (AH IV.6.6). But even in the humanity of Jesus the process by which divinity is made visible is a gradual one. When Jesus was seen God was seen because Jesus was, in his humanity, the image and likeness of God (Dem 22). That humanity will disclose divinity even more when the Holy Spirit is fully poured out on it and it shines with the incorruptible glory of the Father (AH III.16.8). Moreover, since it is only in the incarnation that God becomes visible and audible, it must have been Jesus that was seen and heard whenever God was said to have been seen or heard in the Old Testament. Or rather, since God becomes visible only in the incarnation, in the theophanies of the Old Testament the patriarchs had anticipatory, prophetic visions of God incarnate:

So Abraham was a prophet and saw what was to happen in the future—how the Son of God in human form would speak with human beings and eat with them. . . All such visions are of the Son of God speaking with human beings and dwelling with them. For it was not the Father of all, who is not visible to the world, it was not the creator of all, who said 'heaven is my throne and the earth my footstool, what house shall you build for me, or where is the place of my rest?' (Isa 66:1), who holds the earth in his fist and the heavens in his palm (cf. Isa 40:12), it is not he who would stand briefly in a small place and speak with Abraham, but the Word of God, who was always present to the human race, and told and taught human beings in advance what was to come to be concerning God. It was he who spoke with Moses in the bush . . . [In the events of the Exodus] our own (redemption) was being rehearsed by the Word of God, who showed in advance, by types, what was to come to be.[8]

Through these visitations, God was preparing humankind for the time when he would be visible as human flesh and preparing himself for permanent union with human flesh.[9] Moses asked to see God face to face on Sinai and was told: 'You cannot see my face, for man shall not see me and live . . . Behold, there is a place by me where you shall stand upon the rock; and while my glory passes by I will put you in a cleft of the rock, and I will cover you with my hand until I have passed by; then I will take away my hand, and you shall see my back; but my face shall not be seen' (Ex 33:20–23). This, says Irenaeus,

> shows both that it is impossible for human beings to see God and that, by the wisdom of God, human beings will see Him 'on the top of the rock', that is in his coming as a human being. And this is why Moses spoke with Him, face to face, on the top of the mountain, in the presence of Elijah as well, just as the Gospel records.[10]

In other words, the promise made to Moses on Sinai was actually fulfilled only on the mountain of the Transfiguration.

The notion that Jesus is God made visible is Irenaeus' preferred way of accounting for a distinction between Father and Son, and seems well suited to meet the need to reconcile belief in Father and Son with belief that God is one. But this formulation could easily appear to be theologically unsound to some of his orthodox Christian contemporaries, and Irenaeus also draws upon other explanations of the relationship between Father and Son in his attempt to set out the authentic teaching of the apostolic Church. It may help us to assess his success in this if we look briefly at the diverse opinions about the Trinity which were beginning to emerge in the Great Church as Irenaeus was writing.

FATHER, SON AND HOLY SPIRIT

The attempts of theologians in the early Church to reconcile belief in the oneness of God with belief in a divine Trinity have for long been classified in two broad schools of thought.[11] Theologians of one school are called Subordinationists, those of the other Monarchians or Modalists.[12] Although adherents of one school frequently repudiated the opinions of the other as heretical, we should recognize that both schools commanded widespread support in the early Church. In the 260s Dionysius, Bishop of Rome, censured the subordinationist teachings of certain members of the Church of Alexandria. In reply, Dionysius, Bishop of Alexandria, while conceding that some of his own statements on the matter could be misconstrued, nevertheless indignantly insisted that a real Trinity had to be affirmed.[13] The orthodox theology of the Trinity developed after the Council of Nicaea in 325 rests largely upon a cobbling together of the central tenets of each school. It is as though the later Church was obliged to say that both were right.

The Modalists or Monarchians are so called because they consider 'Father', 'Son' and 'Spirit' to be no more than different modes of being of the one Principle (*monē archē* in Greek) which is God. They regard the doctrine of the oneness of God as absolutely non-negotiable, so that any attempt to reconcile the statements 'God is one' and 'God is three' will have to be at the expense of the statement 'God is three'. Obviously, these theologians drew powerful support from the strongly monotheistic religious tradition reflected in both Old and New Testaments. Some theologians of this school would account for the threeness of God by saying that this is not something that characterizes the essential nature of God from all eternity. Rather, in the course of salvation history, God 'becomes' a Trinity, without altering or dividing his essential oneness. Thus God 'becomes' two at the moment of the incarnation, and 'becomes' three from the moment of the outpouring of the Holy Spirit. In this view, there is no 'immanent' Trinity but only an 'economic' one, because God is said to 'become' three for the purposes of his plan for the salvation of humankind. When the purpose of this divine economy has been achieved God will no longer be three. The one God, having expanded into an apparent threeness, will contract again into his essential oneness. In defence of this view the Modalists were able to make much of 1 Corinthians 15:24–28: 'Then comes the end, when he delivers the kingdom to God the Father . . . When all things are subjected to him then the Son himself will also be subjected to him who put all things under him, that God may be all in all.'[14]

It is very difficult, of course, to talk of a Trinity at all without suggesting three individual, distinct realities, or, as later theologians would call them, three 'persons'. But the theologians we are presently considering were insistent that what there are three of in God are simply different 'modes' of the same, undivided reality. Sabellius, a theologian of the early third century, was associated with this view, and 'Sabellian' soon became a stock term of abuse used by Subordinationists to describe Modalists, who were often anxious to avoid the label. Of Sabellius' theology we know nothing with certainty, but Epiphanius of Salamis attributes to him an explanation of the Trinity which, whether or not he ever taught it, at least helps us to begin to understand how Modalists might have explained themselves.

According to Epiphanius, Sabellius suggested an illustrative analogy between the Trinity and the sun. The sun is one thing, but we can observe three different things about it. There is its circular shape, there are the rays of light that go out from it, and there are the waves of heat that go out from it. Just as a ray of light is sent out from the disk of the sun to give light, and then returns (at sunset?), so the divine Son is sent out from the Father to achieve the salvation of humankind and then returns to the Father. Just as a wave of heat goes out from the sun to give warmth, and then returns to the sun, so the Holy Spirit goes out from the Father to warm the hearts of the faithful and then returns to the Father.[15]

In this 'expansion' of God for the purposes of the salvation of humankind God is not divided. It is because the Son becomes incarnate that one can think of him as something over against the Father, and because the Spirit dwells in the hearts of the faithful that one can think of it as something over against the Father and the Son. But, in fact, there is only one reality, which, without being cut up or divided in any way, expands into a kind of threeness and then collapses back into its original and essential oneness. Modalist theology was represented in Egypt, the Middle East, Asia Minor and Rome, in most of which places it was in competition and conflict with Subordinationism. With some justification, Asia Minor and Rome are thought of as particularly strong centres of modalist theology.

For Subordinationists, the absolutely non-negotiable doctrine was that of a real distinction of personhood between Father and Son, so that any attempt to reconcile the statements 'God is one' and 'God is three' will have to be at the expense of the statement 'God is one'. In their own way, these theologians were just as keen as the Modalists to safeguard the Judaeo-Christian tradition of monotheism, but they thought that precisely this was compromised by calling Jesus 'God' without further qualification. For the New Testament clearly represents Jesus as a separate being, a separate 'person' over against the Father, by whom he was sent, to whom he prayed, to whom he was obedient.

The solution developed by these theologians was to suggest that the name 'god' need not be restricted in its application to the supreme deity. Jesus, or, more exactly, the Word or Son of God who became flesh in Jesus, might be described as god, but in such a way that one could speak of two gods: of God and of a second god. This solution draws upon contemporary Hellenistic philosophy, and has affinities with the Valentinian scheme of the emergence of the divine Pleroma. The reason for the coming into being of this second god was not simply so that he could fulfil the purposes of God in the incarnation, but so that he could be the agent of the divine will in all things, from the beginning of creation onwards. It was by his mediation that the heavens and earth were made and that humankind was fashioned from the earth. He it was who spoke to and was seen by the patriarchs and prophets, and who became human as Jesus of Nazareth. The relationship of the second god to the supreme God was explained in two ways. First, the manner in which the second god 'came to be' was described as 'generation'. The Supreme God, the Father, 'begets' the second god, the Son. The image of begetting implies both that the second god is dependent upon and subsequent to the first God and that there is yet a continuity of being between the Father and the Son. In order to safeguard the unity of the divine purpose these theologians further insisted that the second god was subordinate to the first God not only in the order of his being but also in will. So Justin Martyr maintains that the second god has never done or said anything except that which the first God wills him to do and to say.[16]

Subordinationist theologians set the Holy Spirit in the third place after the Son.

The intention of Subordinationists was to explain how it was that the supremely transcendent, unchanging, invisible, incomprehensible God could first bring about a universe of changeable, visible things and then come to be in that world by appearing to the patriarchs and prophets, and finally becoming incarnate. As Justin put it in his *Dialogue with Trypho*: 'the God who spoke to Moses . . . was not the creator of all but the one who appeared to Abraham and Jacob. No one, of no matter how little intelligence, would dare to say that the Maker and Father of all, having left behind everything that is beyond heaven, became visible on a tiny portion of earth.'[17] The extent of the connection between subordinationist theology and the problem of how a transcendent God could be creative and provident can be seen in the fact that Subordinationists took it for granted that the second god was not co-eternal with the Supreme God, but rather came into being, 'was begotten', before and in view of the creation of the world. It was only when theologians like Origen postulated the eternal co-existence of a creation of some kind alongside God that it was said that this second god, or Son, was eternally co-existent with the Father, that is to say, he had no temporal beginning.

These two schools of thought about the Trinity were beginning to develop in the Great Church when Irenaeus was writing. Can he be said to belong to either of them? This question is surprisingly difficult to answer, for Irenaeus expressed himself in terms which resonate with both of these major theological traditions. Before we conclude that he was too stupid to see the difference between them, or too careless to mind, we should reflect that he was not primarily concerned with this debate within mainstream Christianity. His fight was with those who proposed a complete separation or vast distance between the highest God and the creator of the world. He undertook to show that the undeviating tradition of the Church of the Apostles was that there is but one God who creates all that is and reveals himself to us in love in Jesus of Nazareth. Nevertheless, this presented him with serious tactical difficulties. Irenaeus admired Justin Martyr and borrowed from his writings (AH IV.6.2; V.26.2), but he could hardly deny to the heretics the right to distinguish between two gods and then approve of Justin's saying that there are two gods. Nor is he likely to have wanted differences of opinion within the Great Church respecting the Trinity to be brought into play when disputing with heretics whom he considered to be posing a major threat to the Church from without. Nevertheless, it was from the various and often conflicting opinions about God tolerated within the Great Church that Irenaeus had to try to forge a coherent account of one God who is Father, Son and Holy Spirit.

Irenaeus frequently speaks of the perfecting of humankind by Father, Son and Spirit in ways which suggest at least the functional subordination of the Spirit to the Son and of the Son to the Father. For example, in the *Demonstration of the Apostolic Preaching*, he writes:

> those who received and bear the Spirit of God are led to the Word, that is, to the Son. But the Son takes them up and presents them to the Father, and the Father bestows incorruptibility. Therefore one cannot see the Word of God without the Spirit, nor can anyone approach the Father without the Son. For the Son is knowledge of the Father, and knowledge of the Son of God is through the Holy Spirit. But the Son, in accord with the Father's good pleasure, graciously dispenses the Spirit to those to whom the Father wills it, and as the Father wills it. (Dem 7)

While a Modalist might readily employ a subordinationist framework to explain the relationship of Father, Son and Spirit, it is hard to envisage a Subordinationist at ease with modalist language. A Modalist would have no difficulty in supposing that Father, Son and Spirit in functional subordination to one another are, nevertheless, the one God. A Subordinationist, on the other hand, would identify the one God, *the* God, in the proper sense of the term, with the Father, and think of the divinity of the Son as being of a second order, derivative from that of the Father: the subordination is not just functional, but ontological. The Son remains distinct from the Father, the one and only God; he is 'god' in an analogous sense only. The Subordinationists thought that a second god was needed in order to effect the purposes which the one God, because of his very transcendence, was unable to effect himself. Irenaeus faced a different problem. He had no difficulty with the transcendent God's activity in the world. He took it for granted that God does act in the world, immediately and directly. His problem was rather how an invisible, infinite, and immense God could be seen and comprehended by creatures of finite capacity. His solution was to say that the Son reveals, 'makes visible', not his own divinity, not the divinity of a second order God, but precisely the divinity of the one and only God. The Son is the one and only God made visible, the Father is the one and only God still invisible. To suppose that the Son's divinity is distinct from and subordinate to that of the Father would be to vitiate one of the most characteristic features of Irenaeus' theology: his belief that when human beings cast eyes on Jesus, they cast eyes on the one and only God.

In a subsequent passage of the *Demonstration*, Irenaeus puts forward another account of the Trinity which, while not strictly modalist itself, would cohere with a modalist understanding much more readily than with a subordinationist one.

> Therefore the Father is Lord, and the Son is Lord, and the Father is God, and the Son is God; for one who is born of God is God. And in this way, with respect to the essence of his substance and power, God is shown to be one. And as the one who directs the economy of our redemption he is Father and Son. Because the Father of all is invisible, and cannot be approached by creatures, those who are to approach God must have access to the Father through the Son. And David refers even more openly and clearly to the Father and the Son when he says 'your throne, O God, is for ever and ever; you have loved justice, and hated iniquity, therefore God has anointed you with the oil of gladness above your fellows' (Psalm 45:6). For the Son, because he is God, receives from the Father, that is, from God, the throne of the eternal kingdom, and the oil of anointing above his fellows. And 'oil of anointing' is the Spirit, with which he was anointed, and

'his fellows' are the prophets, and the just, and the Apostles, and all those who receive the fellowship of his kingdom, that is, his disciples. (Dem 47)

In himself, God is one, and it is the one God who 'becomes' Father, Son and Spirit in the course of the economy of our salvation. We need not think of the Son in distinction from the Father except in so far as, in the incarnation, the Son reveals the Father to us. We need not think of the Spirit in distinction from Father and Son, except in so far as this Spirit is poured out on Jesus and his fellows at their anointing. If the distinction between Father and Son arises from the will of God to reveal himself to his creation, might we go further and say that, for Irenaeus, the one God became twofold at the incarnation and threefold at the baptism of Jesus in the Jordan?

An immediate objection to this is that Irenaeus says explicitly that the Son of God did not begin to exist at the incarnation, and was active in the world before it (AH III.18.1; Dem 30). It was the Word, he says, who walked in the garden with Adam; the Word, and not the Father, whom the prophets saw in their visions of God (Dem 12; AH IV.20.7–8). Indeed, he says quite categorically that the Son who reveals the Father has co-existed eternally alongside the Father:

The Son who always co-exists with the Father reveals the Father as he has done from the beginning to Angels and Archangels and Principalities and Powers and to all to whom God chooses to be revealed.[18]

It should be remembered, however, that Irenaeus understood the theophanies, the revelations of God in the Old Testament, to be not so much visions of God as anticipatory, prophetic visions of God incarnate. On one occasion he distinguishes between the Father and the 'Word of God' who appears in these theophanies in language reminiscent of Justin.[19] But we should be careful of supposing that he would have approved Justin's conclusion that there are, in fact, two gods, 'distinct in number, but not in will'.[20] Indeed, he might well have had Justin in mind when he wrote: 'those who say that, since the Father of all is invisible, it was another who was seen by the prophets are totally ignorant of the nature of prophecy' (AH IV.20.5).

It seems that Irenaeus discerned distinct roles for Father, Son and Spirit not only in the creating and perfecting of humankind, and in God's self-revelation, but also in the creation of the universe. Thus he writes:

> in this way it is shown that there is one God, the Father, uncreated, invisible, the creator of all, above whom there is no other God and after whom there is no other God. And, because God is rational, he therefore created what is made by his Word,[21] and, as God is Spirit, so he disposed everything by his Spirit, just as the prophet says: 'By the word of the Lord the heavens were established, and all their power by his Spirit' (Psalm 33:6). Therefore, since the Word establishes, that is, gives body and substance, but the Spirit disposes and shapes the variety of powers, the Son is rightly and properly called Word, while the Spirit is called the Wisdom of God.[22]

Before we suppose this to mean that Irenaeus thinks of the creation as a collaborative effort on the part of the three persons of the Trinity we should take stock of the fact that, when arguing against the Valentinian fragmentation of 'God' into a hierarchy of subordinated Aeons, he insists that God's acts cannot be divided up in this way,[23] that God does not stand in need of any kind of assistance from angels or lesser 'gods' in order to create the world (AH II.2.4–5), that whatever he wills to do he does himself, and all at once, that to say that God creates by his Word and his Wisdom is the same as to say that he creates by himself (AH II.30.9).

Irenaeus' use of traditional language about the Son being born of the Father before the creation of the world might seem to offer strong support for the view that he did acknowledge a real, eternal distinction between Father and Son (Dem 30; 43). We need to set such passages alongside others where he expresses reservations about the use of the analogy of generation as an explanation of the relationship between Father and Son (AH II.13.8; 28.6), and mocks the use made of this analogy by the gnostics, who, he says, lay claim to such detailed knowledge of the generation of the Son from the Father that one might suppose them to have been attendant midwives (AH II.28.6). We should also recall that Irenaeus speaks of the Son being in the Father and the Father in the Son, not only before the creation of the world, but even on the cross.[24]

Given Irenaeus' use of traditional language which might support either answer, it is not surprising that there has been much scholarly debate about where he stood on this question. My own inclination is to say that we should admit that he did not address the question directly and that his remarks which seem to bear upon it have, in fact, another purpose. What mattered to Irenaeus was that God was visible in Jesus. Any suggestion of a discontinuity between Jesus and the eternal God had therefore to be countered. The God who is known, because of the economy of salvation, as Father, Son and Spirit, is the one and only God. The heretics abuse the love and measureless kindness of God in making himself known by taking this as licence to speculate upon the inner nature of God. They blaspheme the God who reveals himself in the creation by inventing another God above him. But the knowledge of himself which God made available to humankind

> was not knowledge of his greatness, nor of his substance, for no one has measured or handled God. It was rather knowledge that the one who created and fashioned us and breathed into us the breath of life, who nourishes us by means of the creation, who strengthens all things by his Word and holds all things together by his Wisdom is the one true God. (AH III.24.2)

Theophilus of Antioch had said that, whereas God had made everything else by a word, he considered the fashioning of human-kind to be 'the only work worthy of his own hands'.[25] He went on to say that while the plural 'let us make' might suggest that God needed assistance in the creation of humankind, these words were not addressed to someone else, but to his own Word and his own Wisdom. Irenaeus in a similar way calls the Spirit the Wisdom of God.[26] It is more than likely that he derived this from Theophilus, along with the description of the Word and the Wisdom of God as the 'hands of God'. This metaphor provided Irenaeus with one of his favourite ways of emphasizing that it is the one and only God that we encounter in the economy of salvation.[27] A potter at the wheel obviously uses his hands to shape the pot, but we do not think of those hands as separate, distinct instruments or tools. The pot is the direct and immediate work of the potter himself. Similarly, when it is said that God fashions the earth creature from clay by his Word and his Wisdom we are not to understand that God's Word and his Wisdom are distinct from him, but that the economy of salvation is the work of the one indivisible God who is revealed to us as Father, Son and Holy Spirit.

It is only because of the way the economy of salvation unfolds that we are able to distinguish between Father, Son and Spirit. If we try to abstract from God's creative and self-revealing acts in the economy of salvation and ask whether Father, Son and Spirit were distinct before the creation, or before God's self-revelation, we will find no satisfactory answer in Irenaeus. For he does not think that God in himself and abstracted from his creation is an appropriate subject for human inquiry (AH II.28.1–3). Nor does he think that it is the eternal relationships between Father, Son and Spirit that God wishes to reveal to us. What God has determined to reveal to us is himself. To do that he must become visible. The Trinity is the means by which he does this. The Trinity is not the object of our knowledge of God, it is the means by which God becomes available to our capacity to see, know, and love him. The ultimate object of our knowledge is simply God himself.

Although Irenaeus tells us that we should not ask what God was doing before the creation of the world (AH II.28.3), I think a case could be made from his arguments in Book II to the effect that he would, at the very least, not be disturbed by the notion that the Trinity did not exist as distinct persons before the creation of Adam. First, there is his strong rejection of the idea that God requires an intermediary for the work of creation, an idea that lies at the bottom of the whole subordinationist position. Secondly, there is his insistence on the simple and non-composite nature of God. In Irenaeus' view, apart from the economy of the creation and redemption of humankind, there is simply no need or occasion, at least that we know of, for God to be distinguished as Father, Son and Holy Spirit. This point is illuminated well in his rejection of certain features of the evolution of the Valentinian Pleroma. The Valentinians want to distinguish between the Father and Mind (Nous) and Word (Logos), but, Irenaeus retorts, this kind of distinction has no place in God, for the Father is his Mind and the Father's Mind is himself (AH II.17.7). Thirdly, he rejects the whole notion of an unfolding into distinct Aeons within the Pleroma on the ground that individuality is a property of body but does not apply to spiritual reality (AH II.17.3). It would be consistent with this for Irenaeus to have held that a real Trinity of distinct 'persons' did not exist before the beginning of the divine economy for the creation and salvation of humankind.

I should emphasize that Irenaeus does not say this explicitly.[28] But one should avoid supposing that he could not have said it simply on the grounds that it does not conform with subsequent orthodoxy. Within its own terms of reference, Irenaeus' theology of the Trinity was perfectly orthodox. He is certain that the God who as Father,

Son and Spirit creates, redeems, and perfects us is the one, true, eternal God. As the divine plan for our creation in the image and likeness of God involves nothing less than the mingling of the Divine Son and Spirit with human flesh and soul, it follows that Father, Son and Spirit will be distinguishable, at least in regard to this economy. Thus, although he understands there to be a real Trinity of distinct 'persons', at least from the time of the incarnation, and although he describes the operation of this Trinity in subordinationist terms, he would not allow that the Son is in any sense a lesser god than the Father, for the essential divinity of Christ is fundamental to his understanding of the work of Christ.

Later theologians would have been worried by the implication that God might change from being one to being three, but this problem does not seem to have presented itself to Irenaeus. Nor would he have been curious as to how this expansion of unity into Trinity took place. It was enough to know why.

Notes

1 AH II.6.1; 9.1; IV.20.6-7.

2 AH II.30.7; IV.20.5-8; 37.7; V.7.2 – 8.1; 36.3.

3 See, for example, A. Orbe, *Hacia la primera teología de la procesión del Verbo* (Rome, 1958), pp. 407, 655-9; J. Ochagavía, *Visibile Patris Filius: A Study of Irenaeus' Teaching on Revelation and Tradition* (Rome, 1964), pp. 67, 69, 90ff.

4 Irenaeus tells us that he has taken the phrase 'the immeasurable Father is measured in the Son' from someone else: AH IV.4.2. For gnostic descriptions of the 'Father' as incomprehensible and invisible and the 'Son' as comprehensible cf. AH I.2.5; 15.5.

5 AH I.10.1; IV.4.2; 6.1 – 7.3; 19.2; 20.1, 6.

6 AH IV.6.6; cf. III.11.5.

7 AH IV.20.7. The seriousness with which Irenaeus viewed contempt of God can be seen in the fact that he considered Cain's cheeky answer to the all-knowing God to have been a much greater sin than his murder of his brother, bad as that was (AH III.23.4).

8 Dem 44-46; cf. AH IV.5.2; 7.4; 9.1; 10.1. Cf. A. Houssiau, *La christologie de saint Irénée* (Louvain, 1955), p. 88; R. Tremblay, *La manifestation et la vision de Dieu selon saint Irénée de Lyon* (Münsterische Beiträge zur Theologie 41; Münster, 1978), pp. 69-76.

9 Cf. AH III.17.1; 20.2; IV.12.4; P. Évieux, 'Théologie de l'accoutumance chez saint Irénée', *Recherches de Science Religieuse* 55 (1967), pp. 5-54 (pp. 24, 29, 32, 39-40).

10   AH IV.20.9; cf. Matt 17:1-4.

11   In speaking of 'schools of thought' I do not mean to suggest any kind of rigorous organizational cohesion amongst theologians classified as belonging to them.

12   Prominent Modalists of the second and third centuries were Praxeas, Noetus, Sabellius, and Dionysius of Rome. Among the Subordinationists were Tertullian, Hippolytus, Novatian, Dionysius of Alexandria, and Origen.

13   *The Letters and Other Remains of Dionysius of Alexandria*, ed. Charles Letts Feltoe (Cambridge, 1904), pp. 177, 196.

14   The last three words are from the Authorized Version, which shows the value of this text for the Modalists better than the RSV's 'everything to everyone'.

15   Epiphanius, *Panarion* 62.1.

16   Justin Martyr, *Dialogue with Trypho* 56.11.

17   *Dialogue with Trypho* 60.2.

18   AH II.30.9; cf. IV.20.3.

19   Compare Dem 45 quoted above (p. 42) with *Dialogue with Trypho* 60.2 quoted above (p. 46).

20   *Dialogue with Trypho* 56.11.

21   This puns on the Greek *logos*, which means both 'reason' and 'word'.

22   Dem 5. The notion that the Father makes beautiful by means of the Spirit what he creates by means of the Son occurs frequently in *Adversus Haereses*; cf. AH I.22.1; II.30.9; III.8.3; 24.2; IV.20.1-4; 38.3; 39.2; V.1.3; 9.4.

23   AH I.12.2; II.13.3, 8; 28.4; IV.11.2.

24   AH III.6.2; 11.5; V.18.1.

25   Theophilus, *Ad Autolycum* II.18; cf. *Ad Autolycum* I.7, ed. and trans. Robert M. Grant (Oxford, 1970). This notion may derive from Genesis 2:7: where the RSV has 'then the Lord God formed man of dust from the ground', the Septuagint uses the verb *plassein*, which properly refers to the moulding of soft materials by hand. Cf. also Psalm 119:73, 'Thy hands have made and fashioned me'.

26   AH II.30.9; III.24.2; IV.7.4; 20.1-4.

27   AH III.21.10; 22.1; IV.praef.4; 20.1; 22.1; 39.2; V.1.3; 5.1-2; 6.1; 15.2-3; 16.1; 28.4.

28   At Dem 43 we read, in the translation of Joseph Smith, 'And that there was born a Son of God, that is, not only before His appearance in the world, but also before the world was made, Moses, who was the first to prophesy, says in Hebrew: BARESITh BARA ELOVIM BASAN BENUAM SAMENThARES, of which the translation [ ] is: *A Son in*

54

the beginning God established then heaven and earth'. This has been taken by some scholars to mean that Irenaeus was content to think that the Son did not exist separately from the Father before the creation of the world: cf. A. Orbe, *Hacia la primera teología de la procesión del Verbo*, pp. 134ff. Other scholars contest Smith's translation: cf. A. Rousseau, 'La doctrine de saint Irénée sur la pré-existence du Fils de Dieu dans Dém. 43', *Le Muséon* 84 (1971), pp. 5–42.

5

The divine plan of salvation

INTRODUCTION

A very large part of Irenaeus' scriptural argument against his opponents is given over to demonstrating that Old and New Testaments do not reveal each a different God, but only different stages of the relationship between the one and only God and his creation. What begins in this way as a fairly mechanical, and, at times, rather naïve, anti-heretical strategy develops into an extraordinarily rich and influential theological theme: a theology of history built upon the belief that it is the God-given destiny of humankind to grow to perfection by gradual stages, and that God guides this development in a loving, infinitely patient, ever-vigilant, and non-coercive manner.

We have already encountered the word Irenaeus uses for this relationship. 'Economy' originally meant simply an intelligent plan (a law: *nomos*) for ordering things properly, especially a household (*oikos*). Even in ancient Greek, the use of the word ranged beyond its domestic origins and came to be used of the principles of government, administration, and so on. Theologians prior to Irenaeus, including gnostics, used it to describe the plans or purposes of God. They spoke, for example, of the economy of the incarnation. Irenaeus, too, uses the word in this sense, and speaks of the various economies of God. But he also uses it in the singular to describe the single, unified purpose or plan which God has for the whole of his creation. This is a significant development in the use of the word, and it is possible that Irenaeus himself, and not one of his sources, was responsible for it.[1] It enabled him to view all the various dimensions of God's relationship with creation as being related to one another: all purposefully arranged by God so as to fit together and achieve a single goal. That goal is the exaltation of the creature formed by God from mud until it comes to share in the uncreated glory of God: it is the coming to be of humankind in the image and likeness of God.

Although the creation of the universe is, like everything else, part of this economy, and although Irenaeus is obliged to stress this when urging that there is only one God who is both Demiurge and loving Father, he is not really interested in questions about the nature or origin of the universe in themselves. The central focus of the economy is the creature formed from mud by the hands of God (AH V.14.2). Everything else in creation derives its significance from its relationship to humankind, for whose benefit it exists (AH V.29.1). For all practical purposes, then, the 'stages' of the divine economy are the stages of the development of humankind towards its divine perfection. The three major stages in this development, each of which has smaller components, are first, from the creation of Adam to the incarnation, secondly from the incarnation until the second coming of Christ, and, finally, from the second coming to eternity.

ADAM

The high 'spirituality' of his opponents provoked distrust and disdain in Irenaeus. It also seems to have heightened his own delight in the material, fleshly dimensions of the human condition which so disgusted them. At every opportunity he provocatively reminds them that the first human being was made from earth. When the gnostics say that real human beings are spiritual and lightsome he insists they are nothing of the sort: they are, indeed, profoundly material and earthy, they are made of mud. One of the ways Irenaeus has of referring to Adam is as the *plasma* or *plasmatio* of God, meaning the thing modelled by God, or the modelling of God. Unfortunately, English has no elegant equivalents for these terms, but an approximation to them can be achieved by speaking of Adam and humankind, as I have frequently done here, as the earth creature. This term is particularly useful in the context of Irenaeus' theology of the human person. It emphasizes the point, which Irenaeus would have us never forget, that human beings are, in their essential nature, material and earthy. It also enables us to catch something of Irenaeus' strong sense of the solidarity of all human beings in 'Adam' (AH I.9.3; V.1.3).

Irenaeus did think of Adam and Eve as real individuals, but he assigned them a special significance which is both symbolic and real. Adam is able to symbolize the whole of humanity in its relationship with God because the flesh of all human beings is derived from his, and is thus physically part of the mud fashioned in the beginning by the hands of God to be in his own image and likeness. Adam is never just an individual for Irenaeus; he symbolizes all humanity, because all humanity is descended from him. Eve is assigned a parallel universal significance, and although this bears upon her being a woman, there is no sense in Irenaeus (as there is, for example, in Philo of Alexandria, in some of the gnostic writings, and in substantial parts of the later, orthodox, Christian tradition) that maleness was a theologically significant feature of the first human being.[2] What makes a human being a human being is the fact that its flesh and blood derive from the flesh and blood of Adam which was formed from mud by the hands of God. This becomes especially clear when Irenaeus discusses the role of the Virgin Mary in the divine economy. For she, and she alone, is the guarantor of Christ's humanity: Christ is a human being (*anthrōpos*) because he derives his flesh from the first human being (*anthrōpos*) by way of the human being (*anthrōpos*) who is his mother.[3]

Generally speaking, Irenaeus' reading of Genesis 1 – 3 is far more modern, far more alive to the symbolic function of the story than the reading that has prevailed in the Western Church for most of its history. Even today, to the extent that there is a popular memory of the story of Adam and Eve amongst members of the Western Church, it is a memory profoundly influenced by the way Augustine of Hippo read the first chapters of Genesis. For Augustine, just as much as for Irenaeus, Adam was a real individual, but Augustine read his story in a much more literal way. The story of Adam's sin and his punishment and death was, for him, a story about the past, but all human beings, as the progeny of Adam, were enmeshed in that past. Although Adam's sin has continuing and quite appalling consequences for all the descendants of Adam, there is nothing those descendants can do about it. All the action happened in the first chapter of the story of humankind and the subsequent chapters have to do with the ineluctable unfolding of the consequences of that action. Christ represents a new and gracious intervention of God in human history, but this intervention does not form a single whole with human history. Rather, from the time of Christ onwards, human history bifurcates: one path leads on and downwards in the direction first pointed out by Adam's sin, and this is the path followed by the vast majority of Adam's descendants. The other path leads up to redemption, and is available only to those on whom God chooses to bestow his saving grace. For Augustine, the fate of most human beings was sealed when Adam sinned, their history predetermined. Because of Christ and the grace he offers, some human beings, and only some, are able to escape from the main course of human history and become part of the history of salvation.

This is in the strongest contrast to Irenaeus' understanding, because, for him, the history of humankind and the history of salvation are one and the same. This path may twist and wander through many detours, but there is no radical bifurcation. Hence Irenaeus is unable to think of most of the action as having happened in the first chapter of the history of the race. Much did happen then, but it was symbolic of things that were still to happen in the future. The human race was predestined in Adam, but it was predestined to come to be in the image and likeness of God. This predestining did not interfere with the power of human beings to refuse to be part of human history, part of the history of salvation. However, for those who choose not to follow the path of salvation history there is no other path to follow, only a blind stumbling about in dead ends.

IN THE IMAGE AND LIKENESS OF GOD

One of the key scriptural texts in Irenaeus' understanding of salvation history is Genesis 1:26: 'Then God said, let us make man in our own image, after our own likeness'. Irenaeus' application of this text fluctuates considerably. For example, at AH III.18.1 he says that we receive in Christ what we had lost in Adam, that is, being in the image and likeness of God. Yet, within a few pages, he suggests that it is because Christ has flesh like ours that he preserves the likeness of the human being who was made in his image and likeness (AH III.22.1). Again, a distinction is sometimes drawn between image and likeness, but not always the same distinction. Most frequently, the image in which humankind is made refers to the body of Christ, both as mortal and as glorified, the model not only of humankind's first formation, but of its final perfection.[4] When the likeness to God is distinguished from the image it can refer to rationality and moral freedom,[5] or to the incorruptibility which will be bestowed on human flesh when the divine economy reaches its fulfilment.[6] Finally, at AH V.16.2, Irenaeus says that the likeness to God was easily lost in the beginning because the Word, in whose image humankind was made, was as yet not visible.

Understandably, Irenaeus' use of Genesis 1:26 has attracted much attention. The Lutheran Centuriators of Magdeburg in the sixteenth century censured him for teaching that man was not created perfect, and that it was Christ in whom the image and likeness of God was first made visible. More recently, scholars have found his use of the text to be self-contradictory and to reflect his uncritical use of various, mutually incompatible sources. Others, again, have proposed elaborate defences of his fundamental consistency.

It would be idle to deny that Irenaeus does draw upon various, and, at times, mutually opposed traditions of interpretation of this text. But it would be unreasonable to conclude that his failure to reconcile the differences vitiates his theological understanding of human nature. Few preachers, or systematic theologians, for that matter, would escape unscathed from an examination of their consistency in the interpretation and application of scriptural texts. Irenaeus was not a systematic theologian, but a polemicist. That he drew upon various exegetical and theological traditions current within the Church of his time is neither surprising nor reprehensible, and should not at once rule out the possibility that his theology on this point was coherent and consistent. At the very least, we should not allow debate about his method or competence as a theological writer to distract us from the interesting and unusual insights provided by his reflections on this theme.

Although he records the traditional view that it is because of intelligence and freedom that human beings are said to be similar to God, Irenaeus also proposes the much more striking and daring idea that a two-fold similarity between us and God is to be found in the human body. When God fashioned the earth creature from mud he did so after the pattern of the body of Christ (Dem 22; AH V.16.2). Thus we are in the image of God because our bodies have been shaped after the pattern of the body of the incarnate God. When the Spirit bathes our bodies with the same paternal light which already irradiates the flesh of the glorified Christ then we will come to be in the likeness of God as well: sharing in our flesh the divine qualities of immortality and incorruptibility,[7] we will have been made 'similar to the unseen Father by the Word made visible' (AH V.16.2). The process initiated when God said, in the beginning, 'let us make the earth creature in our own image and likeness' embraces the whole of salvation history until, at the end of the Kingdom of the Son, humankind will advance to the transforming vision of the Father himself (AH V.16.2; 36.1–3).

Irenaeus has not explicitly brought into unity the various traditions upon which he draws, but his writings do suggest some hints as to how they might be harmonized. If it is the *Spirit* that bestows that incorruptibility which is likeness to God, it was the life-giving *breath* breathed into the earth creature by God that made it like God in rationality and freedom.[8] The rational soul is confronted with a choice between Spirit and flesh.[9] It was through the misuse of the freedom which it received with the breath of life that the earth creature likened itself to the irrational beasts (AH V.8.2), and was thus given over to death, that is, to the dissolution of the body fashioned in the image of God (AH V.9.3). Yet, when the life-giving Spirit bestows incorruptibility on the body, the earth creature will receive the glorious liberty of the sons of God (AH V.36.3). The Spirit who bestows incorruptibility also conforms the earth creature to the very Logos of God (AH V.9.3). The same Spirit which makes humankind like the Son in incorruptible flesh also makes humankind like the Son in perfect rationality and freedom. Indeed, it is rational obedience to the Spirit that enables one to receive the Spirit in one's flesh (AH V.8.2), and hence Irenaeus will identify obedience with incorruptibility (AH IV.38.3).

The notion that Adam was not created perfect, but rather created in the image of God and intended to come to be in the likeness of God at the end of a process of development, is Irenaeus' most characteristic understanding of Genesis 1:26, and the one that most coheres with the rest of his theological scheme. Even though he says that Adam was created in the beginning in the image and likeness of God,[10] there are signs of an attempt to reconcile this with the theory of humankind's gradual progress towards perfection in the likeness of God. The likeness to God was easily lost by Adam because neither humankind nor the divine plan of salvation had yet reached its fulfilment (AH V.16.2). It was necessary that humankind should first be fashioned, and that what was fashioned should be ensouled and thence receive the communion of the Spirit (AH V.12.2). Humankind needed to grow accustomed to bearing divinity, and God had to grow accustomed to dwelling in humankind (AH III.20.2).

God will not be hurried into the fulfilment of his plan. 'All things were foreknown by the Father and will be effected by the Son, in the proper order and at the appropriate time' (AH III.16.7). For this reason, Irenaeus says, Jesus reproved his mother's untimely haste at the marriage feast of Cana (John 2:4),[11] and was unable to be apprehended by his opponents before the hour had come (John 7:30). The corollary of this is that God is patient with the slow progress of his handiwork. When Jesus the second time found his disciples asleep in the Garden of Gethsemane he let them sleep on and take their rest (Matt 26:43–44). For Irenaeus, this signifies the patience of God with the heavy-eyed drowsiness of human beings.[12] This patience, however, will not last forever. With the coming of Christ, the time of humankind's condemnation was fulfilled (AH III.23.1); by his passion Christ woke his disciples from their sleep.

THE FIRST SIN

The sin of Adam and Eve was a sin of disobedience, and precisely the sort of disobedience one might expect of children or adolescents. Told that something of inestimable value (likeness to God) was to be bestowed upon them when they were ready to receive it, they refused to wait. They wanted everything, and they wanted it at once. When the serpent offered them the chance to become like God they seized it. Although their disobedience was thus characteristically childish, and therefore understandable and excusable, it nevertheless had momentous consequences (Dem 12). For it was not disobedience of an arbitrary command, but disobedience of the divine economy itself, a refusal to accept that they were only creatures and not gods, and that likeness to God was to be had only by God's gift, and only when they had grown strong enough to bear it.[13] All of this was implicit in the command of God that they were not to eat the fruit of the tree in the midst of the garden (Dem 15).

Disobedience, for Irenaeus, is the archetypal, the paradigmatic sin. For the only proper attitude of the creature before God is one that acknowledges the truth about God and about humankind — that God infinitely transcends his creation, that humankind is immediately dependent on God for everything. The only proper attitude of the creature before God is one of receptivity and acceptance of all the goodness that God wills to bestow. This preparedness to receive from God is what Irenaeus means by faith: it is a question of *listening*, which is what the word obedience means. Not to accept the truth about oneself and God, not to acknowledge and

62

submit oneself to the divine economy, is to refuse to accept the gifts of God, it is a *non-hearing*, which is what the word disobedience means.

How, then, will that be God which is not yet a human being? How will that be perfected which has just been begun? How will that be immortal which in its mortal nature did not obey its creator? You ought first to keep within the bounds of humankind and from there partake in the glory of God. For you do not make God, rather it is God who makes you. If then you are the work of God, await the hand of your fashioner who does all things at the due time, the due time for you, that is, who are being created. Offer him a soft and pliable heart and retain the shape which your fashioner gave you. Retain the moisture he gives you, for if you turn dry and hard you will lose the imprint of his fingers. If you retain the shape he gives you, you will advance to perfection. The mud in you will be hidden by the handiwork of God. His hand created your substance; it will gild you, inside and out, with pure gold and silver, and so adorn you that the king himself will desire your beauty. But if you become hardened, and reject his handiwork and become ungrateful to him because he made you a human being — ungrateful that is, to God — you will have lost at once both his handiwork and life. For creating belongs to the generosity of God; being created belongs to the nature of humankind. If therefore you offer him what is yours, that is, faith in him and subjection, you shall be the recipient of his handiwork and shall become a perfect work of God. But if you do not have faith in him, and flee from his hand, the cause of your not being made perfect will be in yourself for not obeying, and not in him who called you. For he sent messengers calling people to the marriage feast, but those who did not obey deprived themselves of his royal banquet. (AH IV.39.2-3)

Even in the Kingdom, the process by which God fashions the earth creature in his own image and likeness will never cease, and therefore faith will never cease to be the proper response of humankind to God (AH II.28.3).

Sin, from the human point of view, consists in disobedience to the divine plan, in the desire to take one's development into one's own hands. The goal of creation is that the earth creature should be fashioned by the hands of God after the image and likeness of God. All the earth creature is called upon to do is to become what God

63

makes of it. Essentially, the earth creature should remain passive in the creative hands of God, passive but responsive to the gentle, non-coercive touch of his creative fingers.[14] What the earth creature needs to learn above all is to relax in the hands of God, to let God be the creator. What the earth creature so often wants to do is to take its destiny into its own hands, to establish its own timetable and its own plan for its perfection. Adam's disobedience was fundamentally disobedience to the divine plan, and the same disobedience lies at the bottom of all the gnostic attempts to invent a programme of salvation for themselves (AH IV.38.4). It can be discerned even in Adam's attempt to repent after his sin. He made garments out of fig leaves because he thought these, being more uncomfortable than others available, would be more suitable to curb the rebellion of the flesh. The merciful God provided him with more comfortable garments made of skins.[15] Like all the ascetics to follow him, Adam wanted to conquer his body. His enthusiasm was misplaced. The victory God intends for humankind is not a victory of the human will over the body, but rather a victory of the human body over the Tempter who sought to smash it, and with it the divine plan for its glorification.

Obedience to the creative power of God is the true glory of humankind (AH IV.14.1; 16.4), for 'God is the glory of humankind, but humankind is the recipient of the work of God, and of all his wisdom and power' (AH III.20.2). This glorification of humankind through obedience is also and simultaneously the glorification of God, for when humankind is brought to the perfection for which God intended it, when it lives with the life of the Spirit, when it is truly the image and likeness of God, then it will also be the means by which the uncreated glory of God is made visible to the whole of creation. The Father's light will fall on the Lord's flesh, and its glow will be reflected from his flesh to us, and humankind will attain to incorruptibility, wrapped round with the Father's light (AH IV.20.2). God does not require humankind, or anything else external to himself, in order to show forth his glory (AH IV.14.1). Nevertheless, he has chosen to reveal his glory to his creation by lifting his earth creature up to share his own uncreated life. Freely, and without envy, God bestows on the earth creature the glory and the power of the uncreated; in this, God's love and power triumphs over the substance of created nature (AH IV.38.3–4). God's glory *is* the earth creature made fully and eternally alive with the life of the Spirit (AH IV.20.7).

DEATH

Adam and Eve refused to submit themselves to the process of growth and development which was the only way they could come to their perfection. Satan offered them immediately what God intended that they should have when they were ready for it: likeness to God. This was not Satan's to give, and, were God to allow Adam and Eve to be immortal, he would show himself to have been a liar in threatening death should they eat the fruit.[16] But more, the economy itself would be ruined at its very beginning: for if Adam and Eve were to be allowed to remain immortal after their sin they would have been immortally disobedient, incapable of developing to the stage of loving submission to God which is incorruptibility (AH III.23.1). Therefore, as an act of mercy towards Adam and Eve, especially in view of their immaturity and inexperience, and to prevent their remaining forever disobedient adolescents, God allowed death to enter the world. Death itself was made to serve in the accomplishment of the divine plan, for, by the experience of death, humankind would learn that likeness to God was to be had as a gift from God and at the time appointed by God, and not to be seized by the earth creature as if it had a right to it (AH IV.38.4).

Irenaeus suggests a charming parallel from the story of Jonah. God allowed the disobedient Jonah to be swallowed by the whale, not so that he should perish utterly, but so that he might learn by experience the disadvantages consequent upon disobedience, and so that, when he had been vomited up, he might give thanks to God for this unexpected deliverance and go his way obedient to God. Just so, God allowed humankind to be swallowed by the great monster who had been the cause of its transgression, not so that it might perish utterly, but so that, having received from God an unexpected salvation, it might rise from the dead and give glory to God for ever, thanking him for his salvation and remaining in obedience to him, and never again supposing that incorruptibility belonged to it by nature or that it was itself by nature the equal of God:

> this, then, was the great-heartedness of God. He allowed humankind to endure all things and to come to know death so that it might come to the resurrection from the dead and learn by experience what it had been freed from, and be always grateful to the Lord for the gift of incorruptibility received from him, and love him the more, since one who is forgiven more loves more, and recognize its own mortality and weakness, and understand

that God's immortality and strength is such that he can bestow immortality on what is mortal and eternity on what is temporal, and understand too all the other wonders which God had manifested in it, by which it might come to learn the greatness of God. For God is the glory of humankind, and humankind is the vessel of God's work and of all his wisdom and strength (AH III.20.1-2)

Although this is a much more benign view of God's purposes in allowing death to come into the world than was later to prevail in the Church, it does not trivialize death. From God's point of view death is a loving mercy to humankind, demonstrating the invincibility of his plan for the salvation of his earth creature. From the point of view of Satan, however, death is a victory over the earth creature, a moral victory in the sense that Satan has drawn humankind into his own apostasy from God (AH V.21.3), and a physical victory, in the sense that death will now shatter the body which bore the image of God and was intended to bear his likeness. Irenaeus presents this contest between Satan and Adam as a boxing match, in which Adam's body is so crushed and broken that he is unable to strike back at his adversary.[17]

EVIL AND FREE WILL

Irenaeus, it has been said, is a polemicist who will pick up any stick to throw at his opponents, heedless of the possibility that it might turn out to be a boomerang.[18] One of his arguments against the gnostics had been that the unrest within the Pleroma ought not to have happened, because 'God' should have foreseen it and prevented it at once rather than allow it to happen and then take remedial steps afterwards. If God can bring a certain set of events about at one time, he ought to be able to bring it about at any time. A God who is able to restore harmony to the Pleroma after the near catastrophe, ought to have been able to prevent the disharmony in the first place (AH II.4.2; 5.4). It could be argued against Irenaeus on similar lines that, if God is all-powerful, all-knowing, and all-good, he should not create a world in which evil is found which he has subsequently to remedy.

Towards the end of Book IV Irenaeus attempts to deal with this problem. The occasion of these chapters (37.1 – 39.4) seems to have been an argument against Marcion's contrast between the Law of the Old Testament and the Liberty of the New, and against his reproaching the just God of the Old Testament for punishing those who disobeyed him. Although it has been argued that in these chapters Irenaeus is heavily dependent on the work of an earlier theologian,[19] it is here that the theology of human progress towards a divine perfection receives its most sustained discussion. Against the Marcionite antithesis between Law and Liberty Irenaeus argues that, even in Old Testament times, there was a 'law of liberty', that is to say, human beings were morally free, and were rightly punished or rewarded in accordance with their free moral choices. It was to this freedom that the prophets appealed when calling the People to righteousness, and it lies beneath the lament of Jesus over Jerusalem: 'O Jerusalem, Jerusalem, killing the prophets and stoning those who are sent to you! How often would I have gathered your children together as a hen gathers her brood under her wings, and you would not!'[20] God does not force us to choose the good, but exhorts us to choose it. It is in our power to obey the exhortation or not.

This provokes an objection similar to that brought by Irenaeus himself against the gnostics. God should not have created angels or human beings if he knew they would disobey him, or should have created them of such a kind that they would not disobey him (AH IV.37.6). The rest of the argument is left unstated, perhaps because it was so familiar: if he did not know they would disobey him he is not all-knowing, if he could not do otherwise he is not all-powerful, if he could do otherwise but did not choose to he is not all-good.[21] Irenaeus insinuates into his statement of this objection an unproven assumption, with which he evidently agrees, and which will provide him with what he thinks is the way out of the problem. The assumption is that one cannot be a rational, morally free creature and not commit sin. Put another way: creatures are either rational, morally free, and sometimes sinful, or they are irrational and determined by force of nature toward the good. There is no room for a rational, morally free creature who always freely choses the good. This is a strange view for a Christian theologian to take—but it is one that is often stated as a defence of the omnipotence, omniscience and benevolence of God in the face of evil. It is called the free-will defence. This line of argument is, as we shall see, prone to backfire. Irenaeus does not state the premise directly, but allows it to creep into the debate obliquely. He states the objection thus:

[God] ought not to have made angels such that they are able to transgress, nor human beings such that, because they were created rational and able to weigh things up and make decisions, they immediately became ungrateful towards him, instead of making them like irrational or inanimate creatures which are not able to do anything of their own will, but are drawn by necessity and force toward the good — creatures which have but one direction and inclination, and are unable to deviate, unable to make decisions: creatures which have no power to be anything but what they have been made. (AH IV.37.6)

The argument implied here will work only if it is agreed that God is unable to create human beings such that they always and freely choose only the good. To grant this is likely to involve the Christian theologian in a number of embarrassments. What, it might be asked, of the free, created, human will of Christ? It would not be fair to expect Irenaeus to have asked himself this question. On the other hand, he might have been fairly asked to explain how it is that God can bring it about that human beings will always and freely choose only the good in the Kingdom if he was not able to bring it about that they always and freely chose only the good in the beginning of the race.

It has been argued that there is no logical impossibility in the notion of a world in which all human beings always and freely choose only the good, and that therefore God was able to have created such a world, and ought to have created such a world, rather than the world he did create.[22] Because he wishes to avoid placing any qualification on divine omnipotence, Irenaeus is reluctant to deny that God could have created human beings such that, from the beginning, they always freely chose the good. Yet he does not say, in as many words, that God could have done this. He says, instead, that all things are possible for God, and that God could have offered perfection to humankind but that humankind would not have been able to accept it (AH IV.38.1). While his laborious argument in defence of this fails to convince, he does, in the course of it, have a great deal to say on the necessity of developing, which is inherent in humankind, and he allows us to glimpse the lineaments of an argument that might, indeed, sustain a version of the free-will defence.

Irenaeus' argument turns upon his belief, which we have already encountered, that there exists an enormous and unbridgeable gulf between God and his creation: only God *is*, everything else is in a state of Becoming. In the hands of other theologians, indeed, in the hands of most subsequent theologians of the patristic era, this distinction between Being (which refers only to God) and Becoming (which will always be the condition of everything created) is made the basis of a profoundly pessimistic theology. Augustine in the West and Athanasius in the East were to argue that if a thing can corrupt, then almost certainly it will corrupt. In the beginning, humankind, as it was of necessity in a state of indeterminacy (i.e. of Becoming), was capable of turning toward the origin of its existence and of being thereby reinforced in its existence, or of turning away from the origin of its existence and tumbling into nothingness. The free will of the first human beings was thus the pivot of human destiny. The balance was so finely tuned that the slightest inclination toward evil, that is to say, towards nothingness, would result in a catastrophic collapse of all created reality, an avalanche of all created things, towards disintegration and nothingness. This is the view Augustine and Athanasius take of the sin of Adam, and it has remained the dominant theological view of the human condition, at least in the Western Church.[23] This collapse could be reversed only if Being itself, that is to say, God, were to be joined to the disintegrating created order, and this, for Augustine and Athanasius, is the point of the incarnation.

Irenaeus shares nearly all the premises of this theological outlook and yet he is able to draw from them a far more optimistic theological ground plan. He agrees that God alone is Being and that creation will always be in a state of Becoming; he agrees that free will is the pivot on which the creation can incline towards reality, and be strengthened in its own existence, or incline towards non-being and begin to tumble into nothingness. He agrees that, because creation is only Becoming and not Being, it is almost inevitable that the balance will tip toward nothingness. And yet, whereas Augustine and Athanasius are full of plangent, almost gnostic, lamentation for the fact that, as changing creatures they are removed from unchanging Being, Irenaeus sees in the very creatureliness of the creature, in the fact that its nature is to Become, that is, to change, the possibility of an unending progression and development toward Being, toward God. The creature cannot cease to belong to the world of Becoming, for that would mean it would have to cease being a creature and become God, which, of course, is impossible. But, instead of dwelling on the instability inherent in the condition of Becomingness, Irenaeus emphasizes the possibility of growth and development which is also inherent in it.

It is important to note that Irenaeus does not see this possibility for growth and development as something self-contained within the creature: a principle of self-motion, as it were, towards Being. For Irenaeus, 'to be in the condition of Becoming' is simply the equivalent of 'to be a creature', and therefore the development of the creature, the unending progression from Becoming to Being, is only possible because God is always creating the creature, always drawing it from Becoming toward Being. The whole process of development is identical with the creative act of God. When the act of creating the earth creature is looked at from the earth creature's viewpoint this process of development is what is seen:[24]

> God created humankind so that it would grow and increase . . . In this does God differ from humankind, that God creates and humankind is in process of being created. The one who creates is always the same, but that which is in process of being created must have a beginning in time and a middle period and a time of fullness. And, indeed, God creates well, and humankind is well created. And God is perfect in all things, equal and like to himself, since he is wholly light and wholly mind and wholly being and the fountain of all good things, but humankind grows and advances toward God. For just as God is always the same, so the human being who is found in God always progresses towards God. Nor shall God at any time cease from bestowing benefits and riches on humankind nor shall humankind cease from receiving these benefits and from being enriched by God. For the human being which is grateful to its creator is the vessel of his goodness and the instrument of his glorification. (AH IV.11.1–2)

Throughout this process of development the God who, in theory, could draw near to his creature in all his uncreated glory in fact adapts himself to the stages of his creature's growth. The Word of God, although perfect himself, became an infant with infant humanity so that humankind could accept him in accordance with its own capacity (AH IV.38.2):

> the perfect bread of the Father offered himself to us as milk, by his coming as a human being, so that, being nursed at the breast of his flesh, we might, by this feeding on milk, grow used to eating and drinking the Word of God, and be able to keep within us the bread of immortality which is the Spirit of the Father. (AH IV.38.1)

If we might use a rather crude metaphor, the God of Augustine and Athanasius is rather like a watchmaker who has a splendid scheme to build the most delicately balanced clock. The design is perfect, but the watchmaker knows that the materials available to him are simply not fine enough to make a model that will perfectly actualize the design. Nevertheless, he goes ahead and makes the model, and, unsurprisingly, the material cannot maintain the delicate balance and the mechanism begins to go awry; eventually it will fall apart completely. To prevent this happening, the watchmaker now adds an additional part to the movement, made of a new material, entirely different and unique, which can enable the perfect realization of the design. When this new part is added to the existing mechanism its malfunction is at least partially remedied.

Before we dismiss this two-stage understanding of creation and redemption, with its implication that the catastrophe consequent upon the initial inclination toward evil cannot be completely reversed, we should acknowledge that Athanasius and Augustine were at least trying to offer a theological account of the world they saw about them. If their theology suggests an untidy schema, in which creation and redemption represent first and second attempts on the part of God, and in which the second attempt does not completely reverse the breakdown of the first, this is because they believed that is the way things are. They saw no indication, even after the incarnation of God, that the mass of humanity was turning back to him. Pessimists have always been able to say that they are only being realistic.

Let us turn back to Irenaeus and our metaphor of the watchmaker. Irenaeus' God is more like a watchmaker who knows from the beginning that, if his wonderful design is to work, it will require the use of a special, unique material. Rather than add a new part made from this material at a later point, he incorporates this material into his design from the beginning. Instead of ending up with a clumsy artefact, with bits added to correct the failure of the original design, this watchmaker will end up with the classic simplicity of his original design fully realized and working perfectly. However, it is only at the end that this will be achieved, because the ordinary materials out of which the mechanism is, for the most part, to be made will have to be adapted and refined until they are capable of being melded with the special material essential to the successful execution of the design. Material which resists melding with the special material will be burnt away.

Irenaeus was not blind to the physical and moral imperfection of the human beings he saw about him, but he was able to attribute this imperfection to the fact that the purposes of God for humankind had not yet been fully realized. His optimism was tempered by realism; he did not believe that the will of all human beings would have to be turned back to God before God's purposes could be achieved, but he believed it was in the power of all human beings to be incorporated in the divine plan for the perfection of the earth creature in the image and likeness of God. Those who choose not to be part of this plan will simply cease to be part of any plan at all.

We have seen that Irenaeus drew upon the Platonic distinction between Being and Becoming to describe the difference between God and creation. Other Platonic tags were to hand to draw the distinction more clearly. In the *Phaedo* ideas or essences are said to be 'always what they are, having the same simple self-existent and unchanging forms, not admitting of variation at all, or in any way or at any time'.[25] This description of true Being as self-existent and absolutely unchanging is echoed at several others places in Plato's dialogues,[26] and was to become standard in the Platonic tradition.[27] Philo Judaeus described God in the same terms, and so did Justin Martyr.[28] When Irenaeus says that God alone is without beginning and without end, truly and always in the same state, he may not even have been aware of the Platonic background.[29] Nevertheless, he is fond of contrasting the God who has no beginning with creation which does have a beginning of its existence, and in this too the influence of popular Platonism is strong.

In a famous passage Timaeus asks 'was the world . . . always in existence and without beginning? or created, and had it a beginning?'[30] Although there seems to be a clear correlation between 'being created' and 'having a beginning', and although Timaeus answers his own question by saying the world was created, there was much debate in the subsequent Platonic tradition about whether Plato held the world to have had a beginning of its existence or not. We do not need to follow this argument here. We have already seen that Irenaeus held the world to have been created out of nothing, and for him the Platonic tag 'having a beginning of existence' came to be synonymous with 'created'. Over against everything that has a beginning of existence stands that which is without beginning, unoriginated, which is God alone.[31] So far, Irenaeus is simply using the language of contemporary philosophical schools to account for the distinction between God and his creation, but he adapts this language to take his own theological argument further. Perhaps because the earth creature is so central to his theological concern, in Irenaeus the tag 'a beginning of existence' slips from its philosophical context and assumes a biological significance. In the case of humankind, at least, he supposes, without any argument, that 'having a beginning of existence' is equivalent to 'beginning as an infant'. Contemporary philosophers might have blenched at this carefree skipping across categories, but it provided Irenaeus with one of his most powerful theological insights. Because the earth creature is not God, it has a beginning of its existence; because it begins its existence as an infant, it is necessarily imperfect in the beginning. It needs to grow toward its perfection. Irenaeus conceives the infancy or childhood of Adam and Eve in both physiological and moral terms. Adam and Eve had not had sexual intercourse before their sin because they were still sexually immature.[32] Because of their moral immaturity Satan, already in his full maturity, easily succeeded in tempting them into disobedience (Dem 12):

> anyone who says 'What then? Was God not able to have made humankind perfect from the beginning?' may be answered as follows. So far as God is concerned, all things are possible for him, since he is always unchanging and unoriginated. But things which are made by him, in as much as they have received a beginning of their existence at a later time, must fall short of the one who made them. Things which have come into existence recently cannot be said to be unoriginated. To the extent that they are not unoriginated they fall short of being perfect, for, in as much as they have come into being more recently, they are infants, and, in as much as they are infants, they are unaccustomed to and unpractised in perfect discipline. A mother can offer adult food to an infant, but the infant cannot yet digest food suitable for someone older. Similarly God, for his part, could have granted perfection to humankind from the beginning, but humankind, being in its infancy, would not have been able to sustain it. (AH IV.38.1)

The logic of this is false. It is as though a Michelangelo were to say: 'I can sculpt out of melting butter, but the butter is not able to sustain my art'. Omnipotence is not an absolute quality, of the same kind as unchangeability and unoriginatedness, as Irenaeus wishes to regard it. It is a relative quality: if God is powerful he is powerful with respect to other things, and if the nature of those things limits his power with respect to them then he is not all-powerful. The difficulty could have been avoided had Irenaeus continued the argument that things which have recently come into being cannot be unoriginated, and, to the extent that they are not unoriginated, they fall short of being perfect. If only the unoriginated is perfect then it is logically impossible for God to create the perfect, because he cannot originate the unoriginated: he cannot create the uncreated. It would be easy to object that the logic of this is flawed too, for the equation of 'perfect' with 'unoriginated' or 'uncreated' is simply assumed, and far from obvious. What sense does it make to say that a cat is not a perfect cat because it is not an uncreated cat? To understand Irenaeus' point we need to remember that the idea of 'process' is embedded in the very word he uses to differentiate God and his creation. God is not in a state of Becoming, he is unoriginated, uncreated. Creatures, by definition, are in a state of Becoming. They cannot be said to be perfect (i.e. finished; fully made) until that process of Becoming ceases. When we say that we have finished or perfected something we mean that we have carried through to the end something which we or someone else began. For us, to make something perfect, to finish it, necessarily takes time. In the meantime, whatever it is we are making is imperfect, in a state of Becoming. But is it clear that this should be so for God? Why should God not be able to bring into existence an already perfect creature? Irenaeus' answer to this is that what God has in store for humankind transcends such perfection. For when a thing is perfect, it is finished in another sense as well. It has reached its limit, it has gone as far as it can. It has no future and no present, only a past. God, of course, is not so limited, he is infinite in Being. God intends that humankind should also be infinite; not in Being, which is logically impossible, but in Becoming, which is its natural state. Irenaeus' theological insight pushes the great Platonic distinction between Being and Becoming beyond its original meaning. He insists that the distinction will never cease to hold, that humankind will never cease to be the creature of God, never cease to exist in the mode proper to creatures, in the mode of Becoming. But the goal of Becoming for humankind is precisely this — never to cease becoming more and more like God. The perfection of humankind is to draw near to God and to share in his uncreated glory, especially through the bestowal of the gift of incorruptibility. The goal of the divine plan is that created earth should be so transformed that, without ceasing to be a creature, it shares the glory of the uncreated God (AH IV.38.3, 4).

For a creature to be perfect it would have to be created so, and that is logically impossible. But a creature can exist in an infinite process of becoming perfect, drawing incrementally closer to the uncreated without ever ceasing to be a creature because never ceasing to be in a state of Becoming. In the end, Irenaeus escapes the argument he employed against the gnostics. His God cannot be reproached for not doing in the beginning what he does in the end. For the perfection of humankind is not a static thing, something that can be achieved once and for all. Humankind can never cease being created and therefore never cease to be in process of Becoming, becoming more and more like the uncreated. Even if Adam had been created with the perfection he will attain in the Kingdom, he would still have continued to develop in the image and likeness of God.

Granted that the only mode of existence available to us is that of Becoming, of development, we have no cause for complaint with the plan for our development which, in fact, we find unfolding in history. Morality, like everything else, is subject to this process of development. Irenaeus does not allow the possibility that all human beings might, from the beginning, freely and always have chosen the good instead of evil. As he sees it, the only possibilities are a world in which human beings are free to choose between good and evil and, because of their moral immaturity, do sometimes choose evil, and a world in which human beings have no power of choice between good and evil but are determined by a natural necessity to do good. Of these alternatives it is by far the better that human beings should achieve the good by freely choosing it and striving after it, rather than receiving it effortlessly, and by necessity of nature. For our enjoyment of a thing achieved is related to our longing and striving for its achievement. If we attain the good without longing for it and striving after it we will not enjoy it. Moreover, the power of will and free choice is a function of the mind. If we do not have the power of choice we will not have the power of understanding either. If we cannot understand the good we will not be able to appreciate it and enjoy it (AH IV.37.2, 6-7).

Even if it is inevitable that human beings will sometimes freely choose what is evil, this does not destroy the argument that it is better to be able to strive after and choose the good rather than to incline toward it without choice and effort but by necessity of nature. The experience of evil actually serves to enhance one's appreciation of the good and one's desire to attain it. We would not know how desirable it is to be able to see unless we knew by experience the evil of not being able to see. Experience of illness, and darkness, and death makes us more appreciative of good health, and light, and life. Sense perception of contraries is fundamental to human cognition. To deny this is to deny one's humanity. By taste we distinguish sweet and sour, by sight we distinguish black and white, by hearing we distinguish the differences between sounds. For this reason, God patiently endures our apostasy from himself, incorporating even sin into the plan for our perfection, so that we might learn from our experience of sin that obedience to God is good, and disobedience evil. As this knowledge will be based on our own experience, our consequent apprehension of the goodness of obedience will be all the more sure (AH IV.39.1).

The grounding of this positive evaluation of free will and consequent sinfulness in the distinction between Being and Becoming might, in the end, sustain the free-will defence of the claim that God is all-powerful, all-knowing, and all-good. If being a creature, being in process of Becoming, implies being undetermined to good or evil, if it implies initial immaturity and the need to grow to perfection, if it implies, for a rational creature, the necessity of learning by experience of contraries, then God cannot be blamed for creating us as he did. For it was this, or nothing. It would be difficult to prove that nothing would be better than this.

SPIRIT, SOUL AND BODY

Most of the great heresies of the Christian Church have been driven by an impatience with complexity and untidiness. Christianity, it is thought, will provide a much more satisfactory account of the human condition if it leaves out of consideration all the inexplicable and troubling features, and restricts attention to the central, simple truths. Such a motivation can readily be discerned in Marcion's tidying up of the Christian Scriptures: in his elimination of the contradictions within the teachings of the mainstream Christian communities. Despite all the bewildering detail of many of their myths, the gnostics too were driven by a similar, urgent longing for simplification. All the anxieties that arise from the fact that we are embodied creatures can be swept aside if only one can believe that the spirit alone matters, that bodiliness is not an essential dimension of being human.

In general, orthodoxy resists this drive to simplification. It may not be able to explain how all the parts of a complex reality fit together, but it holds firmly to the belief that a solution which simply leaves out of account the bits that do not seem to fit is no solution at all. Defenders of orthodoxy sometimes err on their own account by over-emphasizing the parts of the truth ignored or denied by heretics and under-emphasizing the parts of the truth which heretics took to be the whole of it. Irenaeus lays so much emphasis on the essential earthiness of humankind that one might be tempted to suppose that he regards the flesh as the only significant element in the make-up of human beings: God modelled the earth creature from clay with his own hands, and it was for the sake of this hand-moulded clay, now flesh and blood, that the whole of the economy has been arranged (AH IV.praef.4; 14.2). Irenaeus himself seems to have been aware of the danger of so emphasizing the inclusion of the body in the plan of salvation that the importance of the spiritual dimension in the make-up of humankind would be lost from view. He finds himself on the point of saying, in direct contradiction of Paul, that flesh and blood *will* inherit the Kingdom of God (cf.1 Cor 15:50), but recognizes that this would be to go too far. We should not say that flesh and blood will take hold of the Kingdom, but rather that the Spirit will take hold of flesh and blood and lift them up into the Kingdom. Our flesh will not take possession of the Spirit, rather, the Spirit will take possession of our flesh and so transform it that, without ceasing to be flesh, it will be radiant with the glory of God (AH V.9.4; 10.2).

Irenaeus finds this point well demonstrated by Paul's metaphor of the wild and cultivated olive. In Romans 11:16–24 Paul had compared Gentile Christians to a shoot from a wild olive which had been grafted into a cultivated olive to share the richness of its root. This metaphor has bothered commentators since at least the third century, because Paul seems to suppose that a wild olive shoot, if grafted onto a cultivated olive, will produce cultivated fruit. In fact, when olive trees are propagated by grafting, a scion of a cultivated olive is grafted onto the stock of another olive, perhaps, but not necessarily, a wild one. For, although a cultivated olive can seed itself, a tree grown from seed will produce inferior fruit, and such trees were known in the ancient world as wild olives.[33] Paul's reputation as a horticulturist is often defended by reference to the practice, attested in ancient authors, of invigorating an unproductive cultivated olive by inserting a cutting from a wild olive into its trunk.[34] But the stated purpose of this was to stimulate the production of fruit on the cultivated tree itself. It was not claimed that the new graft from the wild olive would produce cultivated fruit. Indeed, one ancient author denies that this can be done.[35]

Although Irenaeus divorces the metaphor from its Pauline context, his reapplication of it does conform to the correct horticultural procedure. Human beings who lack the Holy Spirit, he says, are like olive trees which, through neglect, have gone wild and produce the bitter fruits of fleshly concupiscence instead of the fruits of justice (AH V.10.2). However, if they have the Holy Spirit grafted into them they can be restored to their original condition. Just as one describes a properly grafted olive as a cultivated olive, even though the stock is still that of a wild olive, so a human being in whom the Holy Spirit has been engrafted can properly be described as a spiritual human being, even while remaining flesh and blood. Flesh and blood are taken over by the Spirit, just as the wild stock is taken over by the shoot of the cultivated olive which is grafted into it (AH V.10.1-3).

When Irenaeus says that the human being who is fashioned in the image and likeness of God will not be made just of body and soul, but of body and soul and spirit, he means by spirit the Holy Spirit.[36] We will only be completely and perfectly human when we are partially divine:

God's glory will be revealed in the work of his hands, as it is moulded after the pattern of his Son. For it is the human being, and not a part of the human being, which, by the hands of the Father (that is, by the Son and the Spirit), comes to be in the likeness of God. Soul and Spirit might be part of the human being, but they cannot constitute the whole of the human being. The perfect human being is a mixture and union of the soul, which receives the Spirit of the Father, mingled with that flesh which is moulded by hand according to the image of God . . . Should anyone leave out of account the underlying flesh — that which is moulded by hand — and consider only the Spirit, then the thing under consideration is not a spiritual human being, but either the human spirit or the Spirit of God. But when this Spirit, which is mingled with the soul, is united with that which is moulded by hand, by means of the outpouring of the Spirit, then the spiritual and perfect human being comes into existence: and it is this that is made in the image and likeness of God. If the Spirit is absent from the soul then what we have to deal with really remains animate and fleshly, but will be imperfect, for it will have the image in the hand-moulded flesh but will not assume the likeness through the Spirit. Just as soul and body without Spirit is not the complete human being, so, if anyone were to remove the image and disdain that which has been moulded by hand, the remainder could not be understood to be a human being, but either some part of a human being, as we have said, or something else that is not human at all. For the hand-moulded flesh in itself is not a perfect human being—it is the body of a human being and a part of a human being; and the soul by itself and in itself is not a human being, but the soul of a human being and a part of a human being. Nor again is the Spirit a human being, for it is called Spirit and not human being: but the mingling and union of all these constitutes the perfect human being. (AH V.6.1)

THE IMMORTALITY OF THE SOUL

Scholars have disputed whether or not Irenaeus understood the human soul to be immortal.[37] He sometimes seems to be saying that it is,[38] and sometimes that it is not.[39] Here again, the fluctuation owes much to the fact that Irenaeus is a polemicist: what he says is very much shaped by the opinions of the heretics whom he opposes. When he wants to assert that only God really *is* and that everything else that exists does so because and only so long as God bestows existence on it, he needs to say that the human soul, like every other created thing, exists only by the will of God and would cease to exist if God withdrew the gift of existence from it. But when he comes to contest the heretics' interpretation of Paul's saying that flesh and blood will not inherit the Kingdom of God, he wants to be able to argue that Paul cannot have meant, as the heretics say he meant, that only the soul would be immortal. Paul cannot have meant to restrict the meaning of 'salvation' to immortality of the soul, Irenaeus says, because the soul is naturally immortal anyway, and 'salvation' would therefore not add anything new.

Irenaeus' position is fundamentally consistent. When he thinks of corruptibility and mortality he does so in a very concrete, down-to-earth way. The word 'corruptible' means capable of falling apart, or being worn to tatters, or broken into pieces. Strictly speaking, this can only happen to things that are composite: things that are made up of pieces, whether of different things, like the constituents of a clock, or of the same thing, like the atoms of an elemental substance. Only things that are made up of bits and pieces can fall to bits or come to pieces. Mortality is simply a special case of corruptibility: it is the falling to pieces of the union of body and soul. In

Irenaeus' view, only material things are made up of bits and pieces. Souls are spiritual and therefore simple: they have no parts to come unstuck and therefore they are incorruptible, they have no innate capacity for corruption as bodies do. But, depending as they do on the will of God for their existence, they will vanish into the nothingness from which they came should God ever withdraw his will that they exist.

Notes

1 Cf. M. Widmann, 'Irenäus und seine theologischen Väter', *Zeitschrift für Theologie und Kirche* 54 (1957), pp. 156–73 (p. 170).

2 Philo, *De opificio mundi* 151–153.

3 AH III.19.3; 22.1. It is plain from the Latin that Mary was here described as *anthrōpos*. Although normally masculine in gender, *anthrōpos* is used with the feminine article when an author intends the word to indicate a human being of the female sex.

4 AH III.17.3; IV.36.7; 37.7; V.9.3; 12.4; Dem 11.

5 Dem 11; AH IV.4.3; 37.4; 38.4.

6 Dem 32; AH III.18.1; IV.38.3, 4; V.1.3; 6.1; 8.1; 10.1; 16.1.

7 AH V.6.1; 7.2; 8.1.

8 For the distinction between the breath of life and the life-giving Spirit see AH V.1.3; 12.1–2; cf. 18.2.

9 AH V.9.1; cf. 7.2; 8.1–3; 9.2; 10.1–2; 12.3.

10 AH III.18.1; 23.1; V.2.1; 10.1.

11 Irenaeus traces Mary's insistence to a desire to drink the eucharistic cup before the Last Supper.

12 AH IV.22.1; cf. 38.4.

13 Cf. AH IV.38.4.

14 God will not use force to make us obedient to him: cf. AH IV.37.1.

15 AH III.23.5; cf. Gen 3:7, 21.

16 AH III.23.1; IV.praef.4; V.23.1–2.

17 AH III.18.2. Violent as boxing matches often are in our own day, this metaphor may seem somewhat tame. Whatever the actual practice in the palaestra of antiquity, literary accounts of boxing matches present them as occasions of the most brutal inhumanity. See, for example, Virgil, *Aeneid* V.400–484.

18 E. P. Meijering, 'Some observations on Irenaeus' polemics against the gnostics', *Nederlands Theologisch Tijdschrift* 27 (1973), pp. 26–33 (p. 32).

19 See W. Bousset, *Jüdisch-christlicher Schulbetrieb in Alexandria und Rom. Literarische Untersuchungen zu Philo und Clemens von Alexandria, Justin und Irenäus* (Göttingen, 1915), p. 278; F. Loofs, *Theophilus von Antiochien Adversus Marcionem und die anderen theologischen Quellen bei Irenaeus* (Texte und Untersuchungen 46.2; 1930), pp. 24, 26, 420.

20 Matt 23:37; AH IV.36.8 – 37.1.

21 Tertullian describes this argument as the bones the Marcionites gnaw on: 'if God is good and foreknows the future and is able to avert evil, why did he allow humankind, which, by reason of the nature of the soul, is his own image and likeness, to be tricked by the devil and so fall from obedience of the law into death?': *Adversus Marcionem* II.5.1.

22 See, for example, J. L. Mackie, *The Miracle of Theism: Arguments for and against the Existence of God* (Oxford: Clarendon Press, 1982), pp. 164–76.

23 See, for example, Augustine, *City of God* XII.6-9; XIII.1-3: XIV.11; Athanasius, *Contra Gentes* 2-4, 41; *De Incarnatione* 4-8.

24 Cf. G. Wingren, *Man and the Incarnation*, trans. R. Mackenzie (Edinburgh and London, 1959), p. 7; K. Prümm, 'Göttliche Planung und menschliche Entwicklung nach Irenäus Adversus Haereses', *Scholastik* 13 (1938), pp. 206–24; 342–66 (p. 207).

25 Plato, *Phaedo* 78C-D (trans. Jowett).

26 E.g. *Sophistes* 248A, where, again, Being is contrasted with Becoming; *Politicus* 269D, where it is said that only the most divine things of all remain ever-unchanged and the same; *Cratylus* 439E; *Res Publica* II.380D, where it is said that 'it is impossible that God should ever be willing to change; being, as is supposed, the fairest and best that is conceivable, every God remains absolutely and for ever in his own form' (trans. Jowett); *Res Publica* V.479A; VI.500C.

27 Cf. Numenius, *Fragments*, ed. and trans. Édouard des Places (Paris, 1973), frag. 5, lines 25ff.; frag. 8, lines 3ff.; Albinus, *Didaskalikos* XI.2.

28 Philo Judaeus, *De Providentia*, trans. J. B. Aucher (Venice, 1822), p. 9; Justin Martyr, *Dialogue with Trypho* 3.5; 5.4.

29 AH II.34.2; cf. 28.4; IV.38.1.

30 *Timaeus* 28B.

31 AH II.25.3; 34.2; IV.11.2; 38.1; V.1.1.

32 Dem 14; cf. AH III.22.4; V.19.1.

33 Theophrastus, *Historia Plantarum* II.2.5.

34 Cf. Columella, *De Re Rustica* V.9.16; Palladius, *De Agricultura* V.8; *De Insitione* 53-54; W. M. Ramsay, *Pauline and Other Studies in Early*

Christian History (London, 1906), pp. 223-5; *The New Jerome Biblical Commentary* (Englewood Cliffs, NJ/London, 1989), p. 861.

35 Theophrastus, *Historia Plantarum* II.2.11.

36 AH V.1.3; 8.1 - 9.4; 12.2; 18.2.

37 E.g. A. Rousseau, 'L'éternité des peines de l'enfer et l'immortalité naturelle de l'âme selon saint Irénée', *Nouvelle Revue Théologique* 99 (1977), pp. 834-64; H. Lassiat, 'L'anthropologie d'Irénée', *Nouvelle Revue Théologique* 100 (1978), pp. 399-417.

38 AH V.4.1; 7.1; 13.3.

39 AH II.34.2-4.

6

From Adam to Christ

INTRODUCTION

Irenaeus offers various descriptions of the period of salvation history between Adam and Christ. In one place he speaks of four covenants between God and humankind: the first under Adam, the second under Noah, the third that of the decalogue of Moses, and the fourth that of the Gospel (AH III.11.8). In another he speaks of God fashioning humankind, choosing the patriarchs, forming the People, and preparing the prophets (AH IV.14.2). The most elaborate of these divisions of Old Testament salvation history takes the form of an allegorical interpretation of the parable of the Wicked Husbandmen (Matt 21:33–43) (AH IV.36.2). The planting of the vineyard represents the creation of the human race and the selection of the patriarchs, its being let out to tenants indicates the Mosaic Law, its hedging round refers to the demarcation of the boundaries of the chosen People, the building of the tower represents the choice of Jerusalem as the holy city, the digging of the wine press represents the preparation of the People by the pre-exilic prophets for the pouring out of the Spirit. When the servants of the king, that is the post-exilic prophets, came to gather the fruits of righteousness they were rejected; when the King's Son was sent, and killed, the King destroyed the city and broke down the hedges. This represents the destruction of Jerusalem after the coming of Christ and the extension of the promises of Abraham to all humankind. Circumcision is no longer required in the Church because the chosen People are no longer a people set apart; anyone can enter and feast at Abraham's side.

The argument, against Marcion, that Abraham's God is the God revealed by Jesus leads Irenaeus to assign special significance to the figure of Abraham, and to stress the continuity between him and the Church in the one, gradually unfolding, economy of salvation. In Abraham the human race became accustomed to following the Word of God (AH IV.5.3), and Christians are the heirs of the promises made to him, especially the promises of the land, promises manifestly not fulfilled in the lifetime of Abraham and in fact to be fulfilled only in the Kingdom of the Son.[1] Gentile Christians are heirs to this promise because God has raised up sons of Abraham from stones: that is to say, Gentile worshippers of idols have been turned to the worship of Abraham's God and so have become heirs of the promise made to him.[2] Although promised a land to settle in, Abraham remained a wanderer all his life (AH IV.5.3; V.32.2). Similarly, until the coming of the Kingdom the Church must, like Abraham, make pilgrimage with the Word so as eventually to be able to dwell with the Word in his own city (AH IV.21.3; 25.1).

It was not simply because they had inherited Abraham's promises that the Christians considered themselves his children. Following Paul, Irenaeus makes much of the fact that Abraham's righteousness was one of faith, not one based on Law (Romans 4). Abraham is father in faith to the Christians because his religious response is of the same kind as theirs, one of faith understood as obedient subjection to the unmediated saving purpose of God, not obedience to the commands enshrined in the Law.[3] This provides Irenaeus with a means of acknowledging the divine origin of the Law of Moses, while regarding salvation history between Sinai and Christ as something of a detour. Just as Abraham was justified by faith without circumcision so the Christians are justified by faith without circumcision. Faith without circumcision comes first and last; circumcision and the Law occur in the middle times (AH IV.25.1).

The patriarchs had been guided by a divine law implanted in their hearts (AH IV.13.1; 15.1). This 'natural' law was sufficient for them and they had no need of a written code, for 'the law is not laid down for the just' (1 Tim 1.9) (AH IV.16.3). Before he was circumcised, Abraham was justified by faith. His circumcision was a temporary dispensation which prefigured the spiritual circumcision 'made without hands'.[4] The virtues of the patriarchs — the love of God and justice towards one's neighbour — were forgotten during the slavery of Israel in Egypt, hence the need for the Decalogue, in which the 'natural' law known to the patriarchs was written down (AH IV.16.3). Observance of the Decalogue is still essential to salvation, and originally no more was required of the People.[5] However, the worship of the golden calf showed that the People had returned to Egypt in their hearts, and that they preferred slavery to freedom. Accordingly, they were subjected to a 'yoke of slavery': the precepts of the Law outside the Decalogue. There is no difference in the obedience required of sons and that required of slaves, but sons obey out of piety and love, and therefore are given their freedom, while slaves have to be dragged to a state of submissiveness in chains.[6] These pedagogic precepts were abolished by Jesus in the new covenant of liberty.[7] Their only function now is prophetic or symbolic.[8] Jesus did not abolish the 'natural' law encoded in the Decalogue, but reinforced it. Whereas the Law requires that we should not kill, Jesus requires that we should not even get angry.[9]

After the giving of the Law, the next significant stage in the history of the economy of salvation was the age of the prophets. As through the patriarchs, so through the prophets, the Spirit accustomed humankind to obey God, to be pilgrims in the world, and to follow the Word (AH IV.20.8; 21.3). From the time of the prophets, however, God also began to accustom humankind to bear the divine Spirit, and to have communion with God (AH IV.14.2). In the incarnation, the process is taken a stage further. By their incorporation into the humanity of the Son of God, believers possess a pledge of the Spirit which accustoms them and prepares them for the reception of the 'entire grace of the Spirit' (AH V.8.1). Even in the earthly Kingdom of the Son the process of growth, of being created in the image and likeness of God, will continue. Humankind will never cease to be the recipient of the works and wisdom and power of God (AH III.20.2). Since we will never be the equal of God we can never be independent of him. The creation of the earth creature in the image and likeness of God is a process which will never cease, so long as the earth creature, by faith, by acceptance of its creatureliness, remains pliable in the hands of God.[10] Although it has often been supposed that at 1 Corinthians 13:13 Paul meant that there would be no need for the virtues of faith and hope after this present life, Irenaeus was convinced that he meant that faith, hope and charity would characterize the blessed for all eternity:

so the Apostle said, when everything else has been destroyed, these shall remain: faith, hope and love. For faith in our Master shall remain ever strong, assuring us that he is truly the one God, and that we should love him always, because he is the only Father, and that we should always hope to receive and to learn even more from God, because he is good, and has boundless riches, and an everlasting kingdom, and an infinity of things to teach us.[11]

CHRIST

Adam, St Paul says, 'was the type of the one who was to come' (Rom 5:14). Irenaeus builds this idea into his understanding of the creation of Adam in the image and likeness of God. When we think of a scriptural type we tend to think, in the words of the Oxford English Dictionary, of 'a person, object, or event of Old Testament history, prefiguring some person or thing revealed in the new dispensation'. The correlative of 'type' is 'anti-type': 'that which is represented by the type or symbol'. If we are to understand Irenaeus correctly on this matter we will need to be aware that he understood the word 'type' in this passage of St Paul in its literal Greek sense: that of 'impression' or 'imprint'. A *typos* is, for example, the impression made in wax by a seal, or the impression made in a hide by a branding iron. It is in this sense that Adam is the type of Christ — the one who was to come. He does not simply prefigure Christ, but bears in his own body the lineaments of the incarnate Son of God.

Adam's humanity bears the stamp of Christ; it is shaped and defined by the shape and definition of Christ's humanity. When God took up mud to fashion Adam, the pattern according to which he fashioned him was Christ. For it is the incarnate Word, God made visible in flesh, that is the image of God. Adam was fashioned after that pattern and thus fashioned in the image of God. It follows from this, of course, that the incarnation of the Word is integral to the whole history of salvation. Irenaeus does not say so expressly, because his concern is always with the way things are rather than the way they might have been, but it would be thoroughly consistent with his understanding to suppose that the Word would have become incarnate whether or not Adam sinned. Adam, he says, was consequent on Christ, and not the other way around.

The Word — the Creator of all — prefigured in Adam the future economy of his own incarnation. God first sketched out the ensouled human being, with a view to his being saved by the spiritual human being. Since the Saviour was already in existence, the one who was to be saved had to come into existence, or the Saviour would have been Saviour of no one. (AH III.22.3)

As it happens, the relationship between the 'Saviour' and the 'saved' is now conditioned by the fact of sin. Had sin not come into the world there would still have been a divine economy for humankind, with the incarnate God at its centre. Christ would still have been the model of humankind's creation in the image and likeness of God, and he would have offered humanity his fellowship and instruction, as was indicated when the Word of God walked with Adam in the garden, 'and spoke with him about what was to happen in the future, that he would become his companion, and talk with him and live amongst human beings, teaching them justice'.[12]

Adam's sin conditions the salvation to be worked by the incarnate Word but it does not call it into existence. For the earth creature does not come to be in the image and likeness of God until God becomes flesh, until the human being in whose image Adam was created stands on the earth:

> In previous times it was said that humankind was made in the image of God, but it was not shown to be so. For the Word, in whose image humankind was made, was as yet invisible. This is why humankind so easily lost the likeness. But when the Word of God became flesh he ratified both, for he truly revealed the image, himself becoming that which was his image, and he securely restored the likeness, making humankind like the invisible Father by means of the visible Word. (AH V.16.2)

Nor is the likeness of God finally revealed until the flesh of Christ is permanently transfigured by the Father's light and so rendered incorruptible. When the Word became incarnate,

> he received all power from the God who made all things by the Word and adorned them with Wisdom, so that, just as he had, as Word of God, first place in the heavens, so he should have first place on earth, as the just human being who 'committed no sin and there was no deceit in his mouth' (Isa 53:9), and first place too of those under the earth, becoming himself the first born of the dead, so that all things should see their king . . . and so that the Father's light might fall on our Lord's flesh, and

from his brightly glowing flesh come to us, and so humankind might attain to incorruptibility, wrapped round with the Father's light.[13]

Although it is in Christ that the image and likeness of God is first revealed, unless there is a real continuity between Christ and Adam, the purposes of God in creating the earth creature in his own image and likeness will not be achieved. Christ's flesh must be Adam's flesh, for only so can Christ be the 'head' of those who have their 'head' in Adam.[14] That Christ's flesh is Adam's flesh is guaranteed, for Irenaeus, by the virgin birth. Adam was formed from earth before it had been tilled; Christ was formed from the flesh of Mary without any male intervention. Moreover, because she was herself a descendant of Adam, the flesh from which Christ was formed was one with Adam's flesh:

> And just as the first-fashioned Adam had his substance from the untilled and still virgin earth, 'for God had not caused it to rain upon the earth, and there was no man to till the ground' (Gen 2:5), and was fashioned by the hand of God, that is, by the Word of God, for 'all things were made through him' (John 1:3), and the Lord took mud from the ground and fashioned man, so, when the Word himself recapitulated Adam in himself, he rightly took from Mary, who was yet a virgin, that generation which was the recapitulation of Adam. If then the first Adam had a human being for his father, and was born from male seed, they would be right to say that the second Adam was begotten of Joseph. But if Adam was taken from the earth and fashioned by the Word of God, so the Word himself, when bringing about the recapitulation of Adam within himself, ought to have had the same kind of generation. Why then did God not once again take mud, rather than work this fashioning from Mary? In order to avoid fashioning something new and different as the recipient of salvation, and so that the same thing should be recapitulated, by preserving the likeness.[15]

Many of the theories about sexual reproduction held in the ancient world cannot fail to strike us as quaint, and some of them have given rise to bizarre and unwelcome consequences when pressed into theological service, especially in connection with the virgin birth of Christ. There was a widespread view that the embryo took shape when the formless matter provided by the woman

88

was given shape and definition by the male seed, the latter being considered to contain a high concentration of *pneuma* (spirit) or *logos* (the rational, organizing principle).[16] If what is thought most essentially human is the mind, or soul, or spirit, and if women are thought not to possess of themselves enough of the rational principle to give shape to the matter which, without male intervention, will be lost as menstrual flux, it is not difficult to see why women would be seen to have a lower dignity and importance than men. Even if he shared this understanding of sexual reproduction, Irenaeus' insistence on bodiliness as the essential characteristic of the human being led him to exalt the humanity of Mary: she was the human being who guaranteed that our Saviour was a human being and guaranteed that his humanity was one with the humanity we all share in Adam: literally the same flesh.

During the long period between Adam and Christ, the divine and the human were prepared for the union they would achieve in Christ: they grew accustomed to dwelling together.[17] But even when they are united in Christ, salvation is not to be identified with that union. Salvation is a work of God upon his creation, it is not a status of the creation in relation to God. This work of salvation has many discrete stages and elements, but Irenaeus proposes that we view it synoptically, in terms of the restoration of the flesh of Adam, so that that flesh might provoke a new stage in the conflict with Satan and this time defeat him and gain the prize of immortality lost in the first encounter. In Adam's flesh Christ struck back at Satan and defeated him and won for Adam's flesh the prize of immortality:

> because it was not possible that that human being who had once been defeated and crushed through disobedience should strike back and win the victor's prize, and impossible, too, that the one who had fallen under sin should attain salvation, the Son, who is the Word of God, achieved both these things, coming down from the Father, and becoming flesh, and descending even to death, and bringing to its completion the economy of our salvation.[18]

The emphasis of Irenaeus' theology of the human person falls so heavily on the body that one may wonder what significance he assigned to the human soul of Christ, and to the moral dimension of his victory over Satan. Many modern theologians, like some very respectable ancient ones, feel that to be genuine, and of real saving significance, Christ's obedience, his undeviating allegiance to the good, must have been achieved in a hard fought battle of the human will. Irenaeus' strong emphasis on the obedience of Christ as the reversal of Adam's disobedience led Gustaf Wingren to protest against 'any interpretation of Irenaeus which by-passes the need and humility of Christ, and from the beginning simply adopts the standpoint of the victory which has been achieved, without taking into consideration the price of the conflict'. Rather, he insists, 'it is in the *man* Jesus that God's victory is to be achieved, and His humanity implies a long-drawn-out, gradual conflict', a 'lengthy struggle'.[19] Jesus was a human being who 'has to endure the same struggle against evil as we have' and whose victory 'was achieved only in the hardest conflict'.[20]

Wingren is right to remind us of the importance of time and process for Irenaeus, but, attractive as his understanding of Christ in moral conflict might be from a theological point of view, I do not believe it was held by Irenaeus. The moral dimension of the victory Christ won for Adam's flesh is not to be denied. It was, indeed, by his obedience, which reversed and cancelled the disobedience of Adam, that Christ defeated Satan. But Irenaeus does not think of the will, or the soul, of Christ as the place of his anguish and struggle. He did believe, it is true, that the experience of evil as well as of good, and the experience of striving after the good, were necessary for our development toward moral perfection. But, unlike Adam, Christ was not immature and thus easily led to misapprehend the truth and to seek after a false good. He was a human being in whom the rational faculties had reached their perfection. His victory was a human, moral victory, but it was also the victory of a human being as God intended human beings to be, and, indeed, the victory of the first such human being to have existed. Because he was, as a human being, stronger than Satan, who had prevailed over the weaker Adam, he was able to remain obedient where Adam disobeyed. In this way he was able to bind Satan, who held humanity captive, and to enter his house and plunder his goods:

> he fought and he won; for he was a human being in combat for his fathers, undoing disobedience by obedience. He bound the strong one and freed the weak, and gave salvation to his handi-work, destroying death. For he is the most compassionate and merciful Lord, and he loves the human race.[21]

If Christ was superior to Adam in his intellectual and volitional faculty, he nevertheless shared Adam's weak and mortal flesh, and that is where the battle really lay, just as it lay for the morally strong Christians of Lyons, who nevertheless faced the real prospect of undergoing the hideous physical torments of martyrdom. Christ's flesh was weak, and subject to mortality, just as was the flesh of Adam and his progeny. In his flesh he suffered as we suffer:

> if he did not really suffer, we would owe him nothing . . . And when we come to suffer in reality he will seem to us a charlatan if he did not himself really suffer first and yet exhorted us, when we are struck, to turn the other cheek. And just as he would have deceived those to whom he appeared to be what he was not, so he would be deceiving us, encouraging us to endure what he did not endure. We would then be 'above the Master' (Matt 10:24), since we suffer and endure what the Master neither suffered nor endured. But, in fact, our Lord is the only Master, and in truth the good Son of God, and the suffering Word of God the Father become the Son of Man. (AH III.18.6)

The moral strength of Christ's obedience reinvigorated the weak flesh he shared with Adam, and in that flesh he struck back at Satan and won for it the prize of immortality. The work of our redemption is entirely a work of God incarnate:

> the Lord redeemed us by his own blood, gave his soul for our soul, his flesh for our flesh. He poured out the Spirit of the Father to bring about unity and communion between God and humankind. He brought God down to human beings through the Spirit, and lifted humankind up to God by his incarnation. In his coming to us he gives us incorruption, truly and firmly, through our communion with him. (AH V.1.1)

It would be mistaken to suppose that this transformation of the flesh comes about in an almost mechanical way, simply because of its union with God. In his immense love, the Lord did indeed 'become what we are so as to make us what he is', but the consequence of this is that we should follow him as the 'only sure and true Master'.[22] Equally, it was not enough simply that the Word should become a human being: it was necessary that he should pass through every age of life, from infancy to mature years, sanctifying infants, children, youths and elders and offering to each age an appropriate example of holiness, justice, obedience and authority.[23]

RECAPITULATION

A favourite word of Irenaeus for indicating the relationship of continuity between Adam and Christ, a continuity which itself demonstrates the unity of the divine plan, is recapitulation. The verb 'to recapitulate' had its origins in rhetorical instruction. It means to sum up an argument by going back over the principal points or 'heads'. From this it comes to mean simply 'to sum up', to hold comprehensively (cf. Romans 13:9). Irenaeus himself uses the word in this sense.[24] He also has a richly developed theological use of the word. This usage may have come to him by way of Justin Martyr, for the word occurs in *Adversus Haereses* in close proximity to a quotation from Justin, and some have thought that the quotation should extend to include the reference to recapitulation.[25] However, even Justin cannot be credited with the first christological application of the word, for we find it in Ephesians: 'For he has made known to us in all wisdom and insight the mystery of his will, according to his purpose which he set forth in Christ as a plan (*oikonomia*) for the fullness of time, to recapitulate (RSV 'unite') all things in him, things in heaven and things on earth' (Eph 1:9–10). I have substituted 'recapitulate' for the RSV's 'unite', which looks like an attempt to simplify the interpretative paraphrase of the Authorized Version, 'that he might gather together in one', in which the original sense of the Greek may still be glimpsed. This verse of Ephesians was to make a powerful contribution to Irenaeus' developed notion of recapitulation.

Irenaeus understands Ephesians 1:10 to mean that the Word needed to become incarnate and undertake the economy of salvation in order to recapitulate all things in himself. From all eternity, the Word of God has a headship over 'things in heaven'. In order to have a headship over 'things on earth', in order to be the head of the Church and draw all things to himself, he must become visible, comprehensible and capable of suffering.[26] Justin Martyr had claimed that Plato's reference to the world-soul being arranged in the form of the Greek letter X was derived from Moses (Num 21:6–9), and was in fact a reference to the cross of Christ.[27] Plato, he said, had assigned the second place after God to the Word of God, saying he was placed X-wise in the universe. This strange notion, which is not further elucidated by Justin, seems to have provided Irenaeus with another way of describing the incarnation and the economy of salvation as mirroring the condition of the Word in his divine, invisible, nature, so that Christ could recapitulate all things, things on earth as well as things in heaven (AH V.18.3). The Word is the creator of the world; he governs and disposes all things. He is 'crucified in the whole universe and imprinted in the form of a cross' in the sense that his presence stretches throughout the whole of creation, holding every part of it in existence:

> it was necessary and proper that, once made visible, he should make manifest the universality of his cross, so as to show plainly, in visible form, this work of his, that it is he who makes the height, that is, what is in heaven, to shine, and contains the depth, that is, what is under the earth, and, by stretching out, extends the length from East to West, and guides the Northern wastes and the Southern vastness, and calls all those everywhere dispersed to the knowledge of the Father. (Dem 34)

Irenaeus extends the sense of recapitulation as assuming the headship even further by insisting that Christ recapitulated Adam in himself. Just as Adam was a 'head' to the human race which sprang from him, so Christ, the second Adam, is a 'head' to all those who are saved — the first-born from the dead, and the head of his body, the Church.[28] Christ recapitulated Adam because he was fashioned from the very same earth that Adam was fashioned from, and he recapitulated the manner of Adam's generation, for, like Adam, he had no human father.[29] He recapitulated Adam in another sense by retracing Adam's temptation and defeat in disobedience and reversing that defeat in the victory of his own obedience.[30] In this sense, his recapitulation of Adam is Adam's renewal, his restoration to the glory God intended for him from the beginning.[31] Christ assumes Adam's headship by gathering into himself the long succession of Adam's progeny (AH III.18.1). In narrating the genealogy of Jesus, Luke begins with Joseph and works backwards to Adam (Luke 3:23–38). He did this, Irenaeus says, to show that Jesus recapitulates all Adam's progeny and Adam himself in his own person (AH III.22.3).

The parallelism between Adam and Christ is worked out in surprisingly minute detail, probably reflecting an early Judaeo-Christian tradition. It is deduced, for example, from the fact that Christ died on a Friday, recapitulating by his obedience on the tree of the cross the disobedience of Adam at the tree of the knowledge of good and evil, that Adam ate the forbidden fruit on a Friday (AH V.23.2).

A similar parallelism is found between Eve and Mary. Eve, although wife to Adam, was still a virgin when she disobeyed and became the cause of death to herself and to the whole human race.[32] Mary, though betrothed to Joseph, was still a virgin when by her obedience she became the cause of salvation to herself and the human race. Mary untangled the skein that Eve had knotted. Eve was seduced by an angel into disobeying the word of God, from whom she fled. When an angel proclaimed the good news to Mary she obeyed the word of God, and carried him in her womb:

> Mary became Eve's advocate. The human race which had been bound to death by a virgin's disobedience found salvation by a virgin's obedience: virginal obedience weighed exactly in the balance with virginal disobedience. The sin of the first-fashioned human being was healed by the integrity of the first born, the serpent's cunning was conquered by the simplicity of a dove, and the chains by which we were bound to death were broken.[33]

SON OF GOD AND SON OF MAN

The Chalcedonian Definition of the Faith, promulgated at the Fourth General Council of the Church in 451, insists that in Christ there was a complete human nature and a complete divine nature and that these two natures remained completely distinct and unmixed. Although this definition has become normative within mainstream Christianity, we will need to put it to one side if we wish to get to the heart of Irenaeus' understanding of the relationship between divinity and humanity in Christ. For, although Irenaeus himself believed there to be a vast gulf between uncreated divinity and the created order, he also believed that the whole wonder of the economy of our salvation lies in the fact that God from the beginning meant this gulf to be bridged, in the perfecting of the earth creature in his own image and likeness, and in the lifting up of that creature to friendship and communion with himself.[34] It is in Christ that the uncreated and created meet and are reconciled. The uncreated, impassible God becomes a passible human being and reconciles Adam's flesh to the Father, bestowing upon it the divine gift of incorruptibility. Within the person of Christ humanity and divinity are joined:

> as he was a human being so that he could be tempted, so he was the Word so that he could be glorified. The Word was at rest so

that he could be tempted and dishonoured and crucified and die, but the human being was drawn into that which conquered and endured, and rose from the dead, and was taken up. (AH III.19.3)

We must not suppose that Irenaeus is here sharply distinguishing between humanity and divinity, as though they were two separate realities in some sort of loose conjunction. Irenaeus is not saying that the victory, endurance, resurrection and ascension were properly activities of the Word, in which the human being shared. Nor is he saying that the Word was absent from Christ in his suffering. The incarnate Word suffered and died on the cross, but the divine glory of the Word was not evident there. Later in the Christian tradition some theologians would hesitate to say that God, or the Word, suffered on the cross, but Irenaeus shows no such caution.[35] Christ was one reality, who was both Son of God and Son of Man, the unique subject of the crucifixion, and of the resurrection. It is because of this complete union of humanity and divinity in Christ that Irenaeus is able to present Christ's humanity as the means by which his divinity is made visible. What one sees is a human being, but that human being is God: 'he who has seen me has seen the Father' (John 14:9), and this is because Jesus is that earth creature who is created in the image and likeness of God. The humanity of Jesus is the form, or circumscription, of his divinity; it limits the infinite God so that he becomes available to our finite powers of comprehension. Whatever Jesus does or says is done or said by God made visible and audible. This is not to deny the existence of a human mind or will in Christ, a human centre of consciousness, but simply to affirm that that human mind and will is the circumscription of God: through the activities of the human mind and will of Christ we comprehend God in so far as he can be comprehended. Jesus was a human being, but to see this human being was to see God, to hear him was to hear God, to kill him was to kill God.

The interrelatedness of humanity and divinity in Jesus is very apparent in the account Irenaeus offers of the temptations of Christ in the wilderness. This discussion was directed against Marcion and the gnostics, and was meant to demonstrate the continuity of the one economy, in which Adam's defeat is reversed by Christ's victory (AH V.21.1-2). Irenaeus takes the temptations in the order found in Matthew's Gospel, but he introduces material from Luke 4:6 when dealing with the third temptation.

The first thing that Irenaeus would have us notice about the gospel accounts of the temptations of Christ is that Christ was led into the wilderness by the Spirit precisely in order to be tempted; it was Christ, and not Satan, who initiated this renewal of the battle in which Adam was conquered:

> recapitulating all things he also recapitulated the war against our enemy, challenging to the fight the one who, in the beginning, led us captive in Adam, utterly crushing him, and striking his head with his heel. (AH V.21.1)

In the first temptation Christ is tempted to eat after a fast of forty days. His fast contrasts with Adam's repletion in the garden and his hunger demonstrates his genuine humanity. Christ defeats Satan in this first temptation by quoting Deuteronomy 8:3: 'man does not live by bread alone'. That Christ has not come from a Father other than the God of the Old Testament is shown by the fact that he defeats Satan by obedience to a precept of the Old Testament. By ignoring the implication of divinity in Satan's address 'If you are the Son of God command these stones to become loaves of bread' (Matt 4:3),[36] and counterposing a commandment regarding the duties of human beings, Christ blinded Satan respecting his divinity. Satan tempted him on the supposition that he was the Son of God, but Christ merely acknowledged himself to be a human being (thereby giving Satan a basis on which to come to grips with him) (AH V.21.2).

In the second temptation Satan attempts to trick Christ by a lie, just as he had conquered Adam by a lie — promising him that he would be immortal if he disobeyed God. Like the heretics, Satan distorts the sense of Scripture, adding the words 'throw yourself down' to his citation of Psalm 91:11–12. Again, Jesus repulses him by a citation from Deuteronomy (6:16): 'You shall not tempt the Lord your God'. By this quotation Christ again asserts his humanity, and by his humble submission to the command that man should not tempt God he again overthrows Satan's pride. Christ now takes his campaign against Satan a stage further. Irenaeus was, as we have seen, fond of the idea that it was Christ who spoke the Word of God in the Old Testament. He is, indeed, 'the voice of God by which humankind received the laws' (AH V.17.2); for 'the letters of Moses are the words of Christ'.[37] The Word who called to Adam in the cool of the evening is the same Word who 'with the same voice, in the end of times came seeking Adam's progeny' (AH V.15.4). When he quoted the Old Testament, therefore, he was quoting himself. The same voice that first uttered these words in Deuteronomy now utters them anew. When he says to Satan 'again it is written, you shall not tempt the Lord your God', Christ is not simply quoting Deuteronomy but directly addressing Satan, and telling him that the command once given to men is now given to him, and by the same voice. Satan is to understand that he is not to tempt the Lord his God in the man he sees before him. Blinded by Christ's confession of his humanity in the first temptation, and overthrown by Christ's obedience to the Law, Satan had determined to misuse the Law itself in his second assault. Christ shows him that he has not only urged disobedience to the Law of God, but that he has made himself the personal enemy of God in the man he now seeks to conquer.

In the final temptation, Satan summons all his power for deceit and offers Christ all the cities of the world and their glory if he will worship him. This offer also is deceitful, because all the cities of the world and their glory are not in Satan's power to give; they belong to God. On this occasion Christ addresses him as Satan which means 'apostate' and thus unmasks him and reveals his real identity. The three temptations thus show a gradual process of disclosure. In the first temptation Christ confesses himself to be a human being, but does not disclose his divinity, in the second the human being reveals himself as God, and in the third Satan is exposed as the apostate. In this way Adam's insubordination to the command of God is blotted out by the obedience of the Son of Man to the command of the same God (AH V.21.2):

> as a human being the Lord showed Satan to be a runaway slave, a violator of the Law and an apostate from God, then as the Word he bound him firmly as his own runaway slave, and took possession of his treasure, that is, those human beings who were held in thrall and unjustly treated by him. (AH V.21.3)

There is no hint of great difficulty or long struggle in Christ's victory over Satan in the temptations. Christ is serenely in charge of the event from the very beginning. He is never in danger of defeat, he plays with his adversary, and makes a fool of him. If we cannot shed the notion that humanity and divinity are two separate realities in Christ, the contest will strike us as unfair, inasmuch as Christ seems to trick Satan by concealing and revealing his divinity. From Irenaeus' point of view, the contest was thoroughly fair.[38] It was envy of what God intended for the earth creature that led Satan

97

into the apostasy in which he ensnared us. Satan struck the first blow when the earth creature was still weak and immature, before he had time to grow strong enough to bear the likeness of God (Dem 12; 16). As God will not change his plans to accommodate Satan, humankind must be left in bondage until its development has been completed (AH III.23.1, 6). When Christ confronted Satan, he did so as the same earth creature whom Satan had crushed, but now fully mature, now truly the image and likeness of God (AH IV.33.4). Because he is God, 'even as an infant and before he knew good from evil, he did not consent to evil, but chose the good'.[39] Nevertheless, he is also the earth creature as God intended it to be, the anti-type of which Adam was the type, the seed of the woman, who would crush the serpent's head with its heel. As Satan had taken captive not only Adam and Eve but all their progeny, so it was just that Christ should by his victory liberate Adam and Eve and all their progeny (AH III.23.2).

For all the emphasis Irenaeus places upon the obedience of Christ on the cross as the reversal of Adam's disobedience at the tree,[40] it is not altogether clear what the obedience of Christ unto death consists in. Irenaeus repeats traditional statements to the effect that it is the Father's will that the Son should suffer (Dem 69; 75). This would seem to make Christ's obedience unto death unique and inimitable, of quite a different kind from the obedience expected of Adam. For Christ's death can only be willed by God as part of the divine plan for the salvation of humankind. In this sense the obedience of Christ on the cross is continuous with the eternal Son's fulfilment of the Father's will even before the incarnation, administering the Father's plan for the creation of the earth creature in the image and likeness of God.[41] Hence, Jesus did not allow himself to be arrested until the time came which had been appointed by the Father (AH III.16.7), until the time of Adam's condemnation had been fulfilled.[42] Similarly, his passion and death is a manifestation of divine power (AH II.20.3), and the cross itself manifests the headship which Christ enjoys not only over humankind, but in the whole physical universe (AH V.18.3).

Nevertheless, Christ's obedience is not totally beyond comparison with human obedience. Adam's sin was precisely impatience with the timing of the divine economy. He snatched at immortality and likeness to God before he was able to bear them, or God was ready to bestow them. His disobedience is echoed in every human's sin. For every sin is an attempt to achieve human fulfilment either outside the parameters of the divine plan, or according to a timetable other than that set by God (AH IV.38.4). Christ can be the image and likeness of God only because in his humanity, in his flesh, he is totally responsive to the creative touch of the creator's fingers, totally open to and receptive of the transforming Spirit. In this sense his obedience can serve as an example for all to follow. Only by this absolute acceptance of the creature's way of being, this willingness to become what God makes of us, can we hope to attain a share in the glory reflected in the face of Christ. It should not be supposed, however, that Christ's obedience serves only as an example. For Irenaeus understands Christ's obedience to have had a physically therapeutic effect on the sinful flesh he shares with us. Christ came 'in the likeness of sinful flesh in order to condemn sin, and, having condemned it, to cast it out of the flesh' (AH III.20.2). In his obedient death Christ 'cancelled the bond of our indebtedness and nailed it to the cross (cf. Col 2:14), so that just as we were made debtors of God by a tree, so we should receive remission of our debts through a tree' (AH V.17.3). By his obedience, Christ cast sin and death out of the flesh he shared with Adam, and restored it to friendship with God. His 'just flesh reconciled the flesh which was bound in sin and led it to friendship with God'.[43] 'Christ will come again in the same flesh in which he suffered, revealing the Father's glory.'[44]

Irenaeus proposed that when Jesus spat on the ground and made clay with which he anointed the eyes of the man born blind, it was his purpose to show that he was the hand of God which had fashioned the earth creature from the beginning (John 9:6). The man had been born blind not because of his own sins, or those of his parents, but so that 'the works of God might be made manifest in him' (John 9:3). The curing of the man born blind shows that he who formed us in the beginning is the same one who 'in the last times, sought us out when we were lost, took possession of his own sheep, placed it on his shoulders, and joyfully restored it to the flock of life' (AH V.15.2). The whole of this process is included under 'the works of God', the fashioning of the earth creature from mud, which is made manifest in the curing of the man born blind. The blind man becomes for Irenaeus a symbol of Adam who after his disobedience was not able to see God because he hid from him among the trees of the garden (Gen 3:8) (AH V.15.4). The curing of the man born blind is symbolic of the restoration of Adam's vision, just as the command to wash in the pool of Siloam (John 9:7) is symbolic of baptismal rebirth (AH V.15.3-4). In the incarnation, the God who had called to Adam hiding among the trees visits

99

humankind and calls it out of hiding to the vision of himself (AH
V.15.4).

Notes

1 Gen 12:1, 7; 13:14–15, 17; 15:7, 18; 17:8; AH IV.8.1; 21.1; V.30.4;
 32.2; 34.1.

2 AH IV.7.2; 8.1; 25.1; cf. Matt 3:9.

3 AH IV.21.1; Dem 35; 94.

4 AH IV.16.1; cf. Col 2:11.

5 AH IV.15.1; cf. 13.4.

6 AH IV.13.2; cf. 9.1; 15.1–2; 16.5.

7 AH IV.12.2; 13.2; 16.5; Dem 89.

8 AH IV.11.4; 14.3; 15.1. Irenaeus was aware that the Apostles had continued to observe the Law (AH III.12.15), and seems to have supposed
 that Jesus meant that it was to be observed until the destruction of
 Jerusalem (AH IV.12.4).

9 AH IV.13.1, 3; 16.4–5.

10 AH IV.28.2; V.32.1; 35.1–2; 36.1.

11 AH II.28.3; cf. IV.12.2.

12 Dem 12; cf. AH IV.20.4. The notion that the Word would have become
 incarnate regardless of Adam's sin was debated in the Middle Ages.
 Thomas Aquinas said, cautiously enough, that Scripture allows us to
 say only that the Word became incarnate to save us from sin, and this
 does not leave us room to speculate on whether the Word would have
 become incarnate had Adam not sinned. Others argued that the Word
 would have become incarnate irrespective of whether Adam had sinned
 or not. After John Duns Scotus championed this view it became one
 of the points of controversy between Thomists and Scotists. The argument of some Thomist apologists to the contrary notwithstanding,
 Irenaeus' position must be aligned, in general terms, with that of
 Scotus.

13 AH IV.20.2; cf. 20.4; III.16.8.

14 AH I.9.3; III.21.10 – 22.1; 22.3; V.1.2; 14.1–3.

15 AH III.21.10; cf. 18.7; 19.3; 22.1; V.14.2.

16 Cf. Peter Brown, *The Body and Society: Men, Women, and Sexual
 Renunciation in Early Christianity* (New York, 1988), pp. 9–10; Aline
 Rousselle, *Porneia: On Desire and the Body in Antiquity*, trans. Felicia
 Pheasant (Oxford, 1988), pp. 29–31. In the Valentinian myth, the
 female Aeon Sophia was described as having undergone a passion

without the embrace of her yoke-fellow Theletos, and having given birth to 'a substance without form, of such a nature as a woman is able to give birth to' (AH I.2.2–3).

17 AH IV.5.3; 10.1; 11.1; 12.4; 14.2; 21.3.

18 AH III.18.2. The Latin text of this passage has been corrupted in the course of its transmission. The Latin word here translated as 'strike back' is *replasmare*, literally 'to refashion'. But the Greek words for 'to fashion' and 'to punch' are very similar (*plassein* and *plēssein*, respectively), and a confusion between them is evident in a closely similar context at AH IV.24.1. Here the Armenian version has 'God's Son, the Word, in the last times became a human being among human beings and *fought for* the human race, conquered and vanquished the enemy of humankind and gave victory over the adversary to his own creation'. Instead of 'fought for' (literally, 'fought with his fists') the Latin version has 'refashioned'.

19 G. Wingren, *Man and the Incarnation*, trans. R. Mackenzie (Edinburgh and London, 1959), p. 116.

20 *Man and the Incarnation*, pp. xiv, 46, 112ff.

21 AH III.18.6; cf. Mark 3:27; Matt 12:29; Luke 11:21–22. The binding of the strong one became a favourite metaphor for Irenaeus of the conflict between Satan and Christ: cf. AH III.8.2; 23.1; IV.33.4; V.21.3; 22.1; Dem 31. Justin Martyr had considered Jacob's wrestling with God (Gen 32:24–30) as a prophecy of Christ's combat with Satan (*Dialogue with Trypho* 124.3–4). Irenaeus found a prophecy of Christ's victory in wrestling with Satan in Jacob's being born with Esau's heel in his hand (AH IV.21.3: cf. Gen 25:26).

22 AH V.praef.; cf. AH III.18.7; 19.1; IV.28.2; V.16.2.

23 AH II.22.4; cf. III.18.7. On the basis of John 8:57, Irenaeus believed that Jesus was nearly fifty at the time of his death. He claims that this was a tradition of the presbyters of Asia who had been disciples of John. He also seems to have believed that Jesus could not have been a teacher had he not attained mature years, 'the most important and most honourable period of his life'. 'Everyone knows', he said, 'that a thirty-year-old is still a youth, and remains so until forty' (AH II.22.5–6).

24 For example, he says that Moses made a recapitulation of the whole Law in the book of Deuteronomy: AH IV.2.1.

25 AH IV.6.2; cf. Wingren, *Man and the Incarnation*, pp. 80–1.

26 AH III.16.6; Dem 6; 30.

27 Plato, *Timaeus* 36B; Justin Martyr, *First Apology* 60.1–7.

28 AH III.16.6; 22.3; V.20.2; Dem 39–40.

29 AH I.9.3; III.16.6; 18.7; 21.9, 10; 22.1–2; 23.1; IV.6.2; V.1.2; 14.1–2; Dem 31; 32.

30 AH III.18.2, 7; 21.10; IV.40.3; V.19.1; 21.1–2; Dem 31.

31 AH III.11.8; 18.1, 7; V.12.4.

32 AH III.22.4. Eve's virginity is deduced from the fact that, as she and Adam were still children (confirmed by their lack of embarrassment at their nakedness), they had no understanding of sexual generation; cf. Gen 2:25.

33 AH V.19.1; cf. Dem 33.

34 AH III.18.7; IV.13.1, 4; 14.1–2; 16.3–4; 20.4; 40.1; V.1.1; 2.1; 9.2–3; 11.1; 12.2; 14.2; 17.1; 27.2; Dem 40.

35 Dem 88: 'and that he would in his own person fulfil this blessing, and that he would redeem us by his own blood, Isaiah declared when he said "not an advocate, nor an angel, but the Lord himself has given them life, because he loves them and spares them: he himself redeemed them"'; cf. also AH III.18.6; V.18.3.

36 That Irenaeus understood these words of Satan to be a recognition of Christ's divinity is evident from AH IV.6.6, where he quotes them as evidence that everyone who saw Jesus said he was the Christ and called him God.

37 AH IV.2.3; cf. V.21.3.

38 AH V.21.1; cf. III.18.7.

39 AH III.21.4; cf. Isa 7:15–16.

40 AH V.16.3; 19.1; Dem 34.

41 AH V.15.3; 26.2; 36.3.

42 AH III.23.1; cf. 19.3.

43 AH V.14.2; cf. Dem 86.

44 AH III.16.8; cf. IV.20.2, quoted above, pp. 87–8.

7

From Christ to the Kingdom

INTRODUCTION

I have suggested that Irenaeus regarded the period between Sinai and Christ as something of a detour in salvation history. This detour in fact occupied most of that history:

> Faith without circumcision . . . was first and last. It existed in Abraham and the other just people who were pleasing to God before circumcision . . . and it has arisen again in the human race in the last times, through the coming of the Lord. Circumcision and the Law of works occupied the intervening period. (AH IV.25.1)

This dismissal of Israelite religion may strike the modern reader as offensive, but worse is to follow, for Irenaeus could not avoid talking about the Christian Church in ways that disparaged contemporary Judaism. Indeed, the Jews might well have fared better in later centuries had Marcion's form of Christianity prevailed. Marcion rejected Judaism, not as untrue, but as alien to Christianity: the religion of another God, who had nothing to do with the God revealed by Jesus. Marcionite Christianity might plausibly have evolved an attitude of complete indifference to the Jews, so long as they did not try to claim any kind of kinship. Irenaeus' assault upon Marcionism, his insistence that the God of Abraham, Isaac, and Jacob was the same God who was revealed in and by Jesus, obliged him to claim that Abraham was

103

the father of all those who would follow the Word of God as wanderers in this world, that is, of believers from amongst the circumcised and believers from amongst the uncircumcised, just as Christ is the cornerstone, sustaining all things, and gathering in the one faith of Abraham those from both covenants who are ready to make up God's building.[1]

Such a scheme leaves no place for the majority of Jews, who did not accept Christ. Those who boast they are the house of Jacob and the people of Israel are said to have been disinherited of the grace of God (AH III.21.1). They have fallen away from God because they believed they could know the Father directly, apart from the revelation of his Son (AH IV.7.4). Their adherence to the traditions of their elders made them unwilling to accept the Law of God, which would have directed them to the coming of Christ (AH IV.12.1). The Law, as they read it, is like a myth, because they lack the key to its interpretation, namely, the coming of the Son of God as a human being (AH IV.26.1). They no longer offer sacrifice, as their hands are full of blood (Isa 1:15) and they have not received the Word through whom sacrifice is made to God (AH IV.18.4). They were the murderers of the Lord, and because of this eternal life was taken from them. They have killed the Apostles and persecuted the Church and fallen into the depth of wrath (AH IV.28.3). The promise of the inheritance made to Abraham has largely passed to the Gentiles: God had raised up sons to Abraham from the worshippers of stones.[2] 'We have received salvation through the blindness of the Jews, just as they received it through the blindness of the Egyptians' (AH IV.28.3). The reversal of fortunes of Jew and Gentile was foreshadowed, Irenaeus says, by Gideon's laying out the fleece a second time (cf. Judges 6:36–40):

> prophesying that the fleece, a type of the People, which once alone had dew on it, would in the future be dry, that is, that they would not receive the holy Spirit from God, as Isaiah says: 'I will also command the clouds, that they rain no rain upon it' (Isa 5:6), whereas on all the earth about it there would be dew, which is the Spirit of God, which came down upon the Lord . . . and which he again gave to the Church, sending the Paraclete from the heavens over all the earth. (AH III.17.3)

Such attitudes to the Jews were to become commonplace within orthodox Christianity, and, undeniably, they were to underpin much of the bitter hostility of Christians to Jews which was to cast such an evil shadow over European history for centuries to come, and with such calamitous consequences. Still, it would be anachronistic to confuse the attitudes of second-century Christians with the anti-semitism which was to follow. Relations between Christians and Jews were tragic even then, but the tragedy had little to do with race or culture. It sprang from the refusal of orthodox Christians to ignore the obvious facts that their religion was Jewish in origin, and that if they sought to describe or understand it they had nowhere else to look except into the sacred books of the Jews. Irenaeus may have drawn upon material from debates between Jews and Christians, and he himself took issue with Jewish Christians who would not acknowledge the divinity of Christ.[3] However, his own understanding of the relationship between Church and Synagogue was not worked out in that polemical context, but in the context of his own debate with other Christians who denied any continuity between the Old Covenant and the New, and who denied that the same God was revealed in both.

Christian theologians had been profoundly impressed by the destruction of Jerusalem by Titus in AD 70 and its refounding, as a pagan city called Aelia Capitolina, by Hadrian in 135. Some, like Irenaeus, took these events to signify that God had withdrawn his favour from Israel and bestowed it upon the Gentile Church. Others took it as a sign that the God of the Old Testament was not the God of the New. To these Irenaeus replied that one might as well argue that since ears of wheat and grapes are removed from their stalks at harvest time these stalks cannot have been created by God:

> but in fact, these are not created for themselves, but for the fruit that grows on them, and when this has ripened and has been removed from them they are abandoned and thrown away, since they are no longer useful for bearing fruit. The same was true of Jerusalem. She had borne upon herself the yoke of slavery which subdued and made ready for liberty the human race which previously, while death was reigning, had not been subject to God. But when the fruit of liberty came, and ripened, it was harvested and stored in the barn, and from there those able to bear fruit were taken and sown throughout the world, just as Isaiah said: 'the Sons of Jacob shall take root, and Israel shall blossom and his fruit shall fill the whole world' (Isa 27:6). Jerusalem had once borne good fruit, for from her came Christ

according to the flesh, and the Apostles. But, once the fruit had been sown throughout the world, she, no longer fit for bearing fruit, was rightly abandoned and thrown out. Things with a beginning in time must also have an end in time. (AH IV.4.1)

THE CHURCH

Irenaeus' dismissal of the vicissitudes of the Jews after the fall of Jerusalem might strike us as harsh and unfeeling, but it was not smug. He was profoundly aware that Gentiles like himself were latecomers to the feast, and had no title to be there at all apart from the saving will of God. He read in the Gospels that it was the outcasts of Jewish society, the tax collectors and prostitutes, who accepted Jesus when the scribes and elders of the People did not, and these outcasts came to typify Gentile Christianity for him, to the extent that he could scarcely encounter a reference to Gentiles or prostitutes in either Testament without discovering there an allegorical allusion to the Church of the Gentiles—aliens, sinners, worshippers of stones, turned by God into the children of Abraham and heirs to the promises made to him. Thus, Moses, by marrying an Ethiopian woman, made her an Israelite: his marriage prefigured the nuptials of the Word, his bride the Church of the Gentiles.[4] It was in Egypt, which like Ethiopia had always been Gentile, that the persecuted Christ found safety, and there made holy the children from whom he formed his Church. The prostitute Rahab

> acknowledged herself to be a Gentile guilty of every kind of sin, and yet she received the three spies who were searching out the whole land, that is to say, the Father and the Son with the Holy Spirit, and hid them with her. And when, at the sound of the last seven trumpets, the whole city she lived in fell into ruins, Rahab the prostitute, together with her whole household, was preserved by her faith in the scarlet sign. In the same way the Lord said to the Pharisees, to those who would not accept his coming, and who scorned the scarlet sign which was the Passover—the redemption and the exodus of the People from Egypt—'the tax collectors and the harlots go into the kingdom of heaven before you' (Matt 21:31).[5]

Earlier, we saw how Irenaeus interpreted the parable of the Wicked Husbandmen as an allegory of salvation history. This parable is the first of a group of seven which Irenaeus understands to demonstrate the relationship and unity between the two covenants, and the theme of the Gentile Church supplanting Israel emerges frequently in his allegorical exegesis of them. In the parable of the Wicked Husbandmen (Matt 21:33-43) the tenants who killed the servants of the householder and his son are those to whom the vineyard was entrusted 'by means of the Mosaic legislation', while the other tenants to whom the vineyard was handed over represent the Church—the Gentiles who were previously outside the vineyard (AH IV.36.2). The king who gave the Great Supper (Matt 22:1-14) is identified with God, whose city is Jerusalem. Those he invites first are the inhabitants of his city. When these repeatedly disobey the summons, the king destroys their city and calls guests from every way, that is, from every nation, to the nuptials of his son (AH IV.36.5). The father of the Prodigal Son (Luke 15:11-32) does not give even a kid to his elder son, but kills the fatted calf for the younger son and bestows the best robe on him, even though he has squandered his wealth amongst prostitutes (AH IV.36.7). The man who comes for three years to seek fruit from the Barren Fig Tree (Luke 13:6-9) signifies Christ appealing to Israel, through the prophets, for the fruit of justice (AH IV.36.8). Irenaeus' exegesis of the parable of the Two Sons (Matt 21:28-32) is brief and problematical, but a close analysis of it casts an interesting light on his understanding of the Church. The parable is found in the RSV and in most modern Bibles in the following form:

'What do you think? A man had two sons; and he went to the first and said, "Son, go and work in the vineyard to-day". And he answered, "I will not"; but afterward he repented and went. And he went to the second and said the same; and he answered, "I go, Sir," but did not go. Which of the two did the will of his father?' They said, 'The first.' Jesus said to them, 'Truly, I say to you, the tax collectors and the harlots go into the kingdom of God before you. For John came to you in the way of righteousness, and you did not believe him, but the tax collectors and the harlots believed him; and even when you saw it, you did not afterward repent and believe him.'

While the parable appears to make good sense in this form, and has strong support from the manuscript tradition of the Greek New Testament, this is not the only form in which the parable is preserved in the textual tradition. Some manuscripts have the first son saying, 'I go', and doing nothing, and the second son saying 'No', but afterward repenting and going. In this case it is the second son who is said to do the father's will. In this form the parable makes the same general sense as in the first form. But there is yet a third group of manuscript witnesses in which, as in the first form, the first son says 'No', but afterwards repents and goes, and the second son says 'I go', but does not. In this third form, however, it is the second son who, paradoxically, is said to have done the Father's will. Although it had been known as early as Jerome that such textual variants existed, and although the third form of the parable has been dismissed as 'nonsensical', it was, oddly enough, this form of the parable that established itself in the Western Church and maintained its position in the Latin Vulgate until very recent times.[6] Irenaeus does not quote the parable in full, but it is clear that he read it in this form, and that he was familiar with an elaborate theological exegesis of it.

> And the parable of the two sons, who are sent into the vineyard, one of whom defied his father and repented afterwards, when repentance was of no avail to him, while the other promised to go, giving his word to his father at once, but did not go in fact (for every man is a liar, and it is one thing to will something but another to carry it through) showed there to be one and the same Father. (AH IV.36.8)

The first and the second son represent Israel and the Church, the two sons of the one God. Earlier in Book IV, and for exactly the same purpose, Rebecca's twin pregnancy had been described as a prophecy of the two peoples, one elder and one younger, one slave, the other free, yet both sons of the same father. Similarly, Jacob supplanted his elder brother and received the rights of the first-born when Esau had spoken slightingly of them and, just so, the younger people accepted Christ, the first-born, when the elder people had rejected him with the words 'we have no king but Caesar'. In Christ, the younger people stole from the Father the blessings of the elder people, just as Jacob stole the blessings of Esau.[7] Jacob begat children of Leah and Rachel, but loved the latter, so Christ presented sons to the Father from two peoples, giving the Spirit to all alike, yet doing everything for the sake of the younger one, the lovely-eyed Rachel, who prefigured the Church for which Christ suffered.[8]

Irenaeus finds the key to the interpretation of the parable of the

Two Sons in the words of Jesus to the 'chief priests and elders of the people' (Matt 21:23): 'For John came to you in the way of righteousness, and you did not believe him, but the tax collectors and harlots believed him' (Matt 21:32). The son whom the father approached first represents the chief priests and the elders, the second son represents the tax collectors and prostitutes; so it is that the Church of the Gentiles goes before Israel into the Kingdom. In the parable of the Prodigal Son it was the younger son, who spent his wealth amongst prostitutes in a far land, who was favoured by his father. It was the tax collector rather than the Pharisee who went down to his house justified. Similarly, it was the second son, the one who said he would go but did not, who did the will of the father.

The excuse given for the second son's not going when he said he would does not advocate lip service in place of real obedience to the command of God. It points to Irenaeus' view that faith itself, the ready responsiveness to the creative power of God, is all that creatures are actually expected to have. The actual 'doing' is in the hands of God:

> to make is proper to the kindness of God, to be made is proper to the nature of humankind. If you give him what is yours, that is faith in him and subjection, you will become the recipient of his handiwork and a perfect work of God. (AH IV.39.2)

Irenaeus' own church of Lyons was, in fact, considerably more lenient than some other Christian communities of the second and third centuries when it came to dealing with those who sought reconciliation after lapsing in time of persecution.[9] But Irenaeus is not advocating a lax, much less an antinomian, position. Holiness is a mark of the Church, and is expected of its members: they no less than the people of the Old Covenant will be expected to produce the fruits of justice when these are called for. But holiness and justice are not *achievements* of the Church or of its members. They follow from faith in the sense that it is only because of this obedience, this receptiveness to the creative touch of God, that God can bestow such beauty on his creatures.

The Gospel does not offer Gentiles a new dispensation of salvation. There is only one economy of salvation, and the Gentiles will legitimately inherit the promises made to Abraham because Christ has made them the adopted children of Abraham (AH IV.8.1). He has called them to Abraham's faith; they are to 'shine as lights in the world' (Phil 2:15), for they are the 'light of the world' (Matt 5:14).

In this way is the prophecy fulfilled that Abraham's descendants would be as numerous as the stars of heaven (Gen 15:5; 22:17) (AH IV.7.3). Men will come from East and West and from North and South to sit at table with Abraham and Isaac and Jacob in the Kingdom of Heaven, while the Jews themselves will be excluded.[10] Irenaeus even supposes that the Word revealed to Abraham that his own coming as a human being would be the means by which Abraham's seed would become as the stars of heaven. He puts together Matthew 13:17 ('Truly I say to you, many prophets and righteous men longed to see what you see and did not see it, and to hear what you hear and did not hear it') and John 8:56 ('Your father Abraham rejoiced that he was to see my day; he saw it and was glad'). Abraham, Irenaeus says, longed to see the day of the Lord's coming so that he might himself embrace the Christ, and, having seen this day prophetically, by means of the Spirit, he rejoiced. His joy passed down to his descendants who watched for the coming of Christ. It was expressed in the songs of those who saw him and held him: in the *Nunc dimittis* of Simeon and in the *Magnificat* of Elizabeth;[11] from them it echoes back along the line of Abraham's progeny to the patriarch himself (AH IV.7.1).

ADOPTION

Gentile Christians may have displaced the Jewish people as heirs to the promises made to Abraham, but they have not yet come into that inheritance. Like Abraham, they are still wanderers. Thus Irenaeus will not present the Church as the fulfilment of the Old Testament, but as the last, and relatively short, stage in the pilgrimage of faith. Christ is the goal of human history, but he will not have fully revealed himself as the image and likeness of God until his coming in glory. The Church is the body of Christ, the new Adam, being fashioned in the image and likeness of God (AH IV.37.7). However, salvation history will reach its climax not in the Church, but in the Kingdom of the Son. It is there that the promises made to Abraham will finally be fulfilled, and in order to enjoy them one must be adopted to sonship not only of Abraham, but of God himself (AH V.32.2). This adoption to sonship of God is achieved by incorporation into Christ as the second Adam, for it is not as individuals that human beings are fashioned in the image and likeness of God, but precisely as members of the Church, members of that body of which Christ is the head.[12]

110

The word 'adoption', especially when used theologically, nearly always suggests a contrast between genuine and reputed sonship, to the detriment of the latter. In the Arian crisis of the fourth century ferocious battles were to rage within the Church about whether Christ was the Son of God by nature or by adoption. It is important to note that Irenaeus does not understand adopted sonship in this manner. The English verb 'adopt' comes directly from the Latin, where its primary meaning is 'to select something for oneself'. It is easy to see how this soon came to be applied to the adoption of children, but, even in English, the concept of adoption is not restricted to such relationships. One can adopt a point of view, an attitude and so on. Irenaeus' word for 'adoption' was *huiothesia*: literally, 'establishment as a son'. This word thus has a far more restricted application than its English and Latin equivalents, and a far stronger sense. 'Adoption' in Irenaeus' language does not carry the same suggestion of second-class sonship that the Latin and English words often do carry.

A discussion of different types of sonship occurs towards the end of *Adversus Haereses* Book IV, where Irenaeus tells us he is drawing on the work of one of his predecessors (AH IV.41.2). The discussion is introduced in order to counter the misinterpretation of scriptural texts which speak of human beings as sons of the Evil One or a brood of vipers (Matt 13:38; 23:33). We do not know who it is that Irenaeus is following here, nor the original context of the distinction he proposes. Quite possibly, it was christological. There are significant differences in the way the passage has been transmitted in the Latin and Armenian versions, the result, it seems, of theological qualms on the part of translators or copyists at work after the Arian crisis had taught orthodox Christians to speak more cautiously about different types of sonship. Which of the versions suffered the more from this theological retouching is open to question. Dom Adelin Rousseau leans more towards the Armenian in his translation for the Sources chrétiennes edition. The following résumé gives more preference to the Latin version.

Natural sonship is the relationship between a son and the father who begets him. But there are also two kinds of analogical sonship: two relationships in virtue of which one person may be regarded as son to another. The first of these is a quasi-natural sonship and applies only to the relationship between human beings and the God who created them. Because all human beings are created by God they are all entitled to be called sons of God by nature. Therefore, if human beings are called sons of the Evil One it cannot mean that

111

they have been created by the Evil One. The other kind of analogical sonship arises from the relationship between a pupil and his teacher. Human beings will be sons of God in this sense only so long as they maintain an attitude of filial obedience toward God; so long as they believe in him and do his will. It is when they disobey God and obey the Evil One that they are said to be, in this sense, sons of the Evil One (AH IV.41.2–3).

A natural son can be disinherited, his sonship can be set aside, should he cease to be obedient to his father. Similarly, human beings, while naturally sons of God because created by him, will only be regarded as sons, and receive their inheritance of incorruptibility, so long as they remain in filial obedience to God. Although this 'ethical' dimension of sonship is extremely important to Irenaeus it is not simply this that he has in mind when he speaks of our being adopted as sons of God. We cannot simply acquire this adopted sonship by our own effort, by being obedient to the God who created us. Adoptive sonship is a gift from God, bestowed on us in Christ.[13] As such it is of a far higher order than the natural sonship we have as God's creatures. For the creator is a 'merciful, forgiving, most gentle, kind and just God of all, of Jews and Gentiles and believers'. But, while 'to the Jews he was as a Lord and Lawgiver', and 'to the Gentiles as a maker and creator', to believers he is a Father, 'for in the end of times he has opened the covenant of adoption' (Dem 8). This adopted sonship obviously implies filial obedience, but it is not simply a restoration of a right relationship between God and his creatures. It is an incorporation into the natural sonship which is Christ's as the only *begotten* son of God. Obviously, as creatures, we cannot be begotten of God in the way the divine Son is, but when Irenaeus speaks of our adoption as sons of God he does not mean that God simply chooses to look upon us as though we were his sons, he means that God has *established us* as sons by incorporating us into his only begotten Son. For this reason Irenaeus does not hesitate to say that when the Psalmist speaks of the 'assembly of the gods' he means by 'gods' 'the Father, the Son and those who have been established as sons, that is, those who constitute the Church'.[14]

BAPTISM

Irenaeus was fond of describing the Spirit as the water of life, and it is clear that he understood baptism as the means by which believers are adopted to sonship with Christ.[15] As always, his focus is on the body. It is this that needs to be cleansed, and reconciled to God. It is this that needs to be made solid against its natural tendency to disintegrate, it is this that needs to be anointed, so as to shine with the glory of God.

In baptism, sins are washed away, because by baptism believers are incorporated into the 'just' flesh of Christ, which has been washed with his own blood, from which sin has been cast out, and which has been reconciled to the Father.[16] The Spirit, which gives unity, form, and beauty to the created order, in baptism bestows on the earth creature the unity, form, and cohesion which enables it to endure everlastingly in the image and likeness of God. It was with this Spirit that Jesus was anointed in the Jordan to become the Christ, the Anointed One, when the Spirit came down upon him so as to

grow accustomed with him to dwell amongst the human race and to rest upon human beings and to dwell within what God had modelled, working the Father's will in them and renewing them from oldness to newness in Christ.[17]

This same Spirit was poured out on the disciples at Pentecost and

gathered into unity all the distant tribes and offered to the Father the first-fruit of all the Gentiles, just as the Lord had promised to send the Paraclete, who would make us fit for God. For just as a lump of dough or a loaf of bread cannot be made from dry flour without its being moistened, so neither could we who were many be made one in Christ without the water from heaven. Just as dry earth, unless it is moistened, will not give fruit, so we, who formerly were dry wood, would never have produced the fruit of life without the gracious rain from above. Our bodies have received the wholeness of incorruption from baptismal washing, our souls have received it from the Spirit. (AH III.17.2)

The Spirit is breathed into the Church as the breath of life was breathed into the earth creature. To be cut off from the Church is to have no access to the limpid stream which flows from the body of Christ. For, 'where the Church is, there is the Spirit of God, and where the Spirit of God is, there is the Church, and every grace' (AH III.24.1–2).

Irenaeus records the existence of charismatic gifts, such as speaking in tongues, prophecy, divining of secrets, exorcism, visions, healings, and raising the dead to life (AH II.32.4; V.6.1). Although he approves these phenomena, so long as they are genuine and beneficial to others, he makes no claim to have received such gifts himself.

EUCHARIST

The incarnation of the Word signifies that the perfection of humankind is approaching its final stage. The novelty of heresy shows that the Church is no longer young (AH III.4.3). The period of preparation is nearly over, the fruits of righteousness will soon be harvested (AH II.22.2). In the short time remaining the Church must nourish and strengthen her children, especially in the prospect of martyrdom, which is a mark of her authenticity, and against the heretics who would deprive them of their inheritance.[18]

The chief means by which members of the Church are prepared for their physical perfection is in the reception of the Eucharist. As the Eucharist *is* the body and blood of Christ, it is, like the incarnate Word, a union and commingling of earthly flesh and divine Spirit.[19] When believers partake of the Eucharist their flesh and blood are strengthened by the flesh and blood of Christ, and thus made ready for incorruptibility:

> we offer to him what is his own, fittingly proclaiming the communion and union of flesh and Spirit. For just as bread from the earth, when it has received the invocation (epiclesis) of God, is no longer ordinary bread, but Eucharist, subsisting in the union of two things, one earthly and the other heavenly, just so, when our bodies receive the Eucharist, they are no longer corruptible, but have the hope of resurrection. (AH IV.18.4–5)

It is evident that Irenaeus has a strong sense of the real, physical, presence of Christ in the Eucharist. He does not address the question of whether bread and wine are 'changed' into the body and blood of Christ. His interest is much rather engaged by the change effected in the body and blood of the recipient. For he understands the Eucharistic elements to act upon the recipient in a directly physical way:

> Given that the cup which has been mixed and the bread that has been manufactured receive the Word of God and become the Eucharist—the body and blood of Christ—and that the

114

substance of our flesh has grown and been strengthened out of these, how can they deny that the flesh which has been nourished by the body and blood of Christ, and is part of him, is capable of receiving God's gift of eternal life? When the blessed Apostle says in the Letter to the Ephesians 'for we are members of his body and of his flesh and of his bones' (Eph 5:30), he is not speaking of some spiritual and invisible human being – 'for a spirit has neither bones nor flesh' (Luke 24:39) – but of a genuine human being, made up of flesh and nerves and bones, which is nourished from the cup which is his blood and replenished by the bread which is his body.[20]

The union and intermingling of matter and Spirit in the earth creature fashioned in the image and likeness of God is the whole focus of the divine economy. This economy will not be achieved until after the resurrection of the just, when their bodies will be bathed in the reflected glory of the Father's light shining from the body of Jesus. Between the manifestation of this mingling of earthly and spiritual in the incarnation, and its realization in their own bodies at the resurrection, the bodies of believers are sustained and prepared by that mingling of flesh and Spirit which is the body and blood of Christ in the Eucharist.

Irenaeus finds in the Eucharist an eloquent demonstration of one of the central themes of his theology, that destined though we may be for union with the divine, our earthly nature will never cease to be earthly, even when it is resplendent with the glory of the Spirit:

The wood of the vine, planted in the earth, bore fruit in its own time. The grain of wheat, after falling on the earth and perishing, was raised up manifold by the Spirit of God which holds all things in being. Wisdom made this produce useful to human beings, and then, after receiving the Word of God, they became the Eucharist, which is the body and blood of Christ. In the same way, our bodies, which have been nourished by the Eucharist, after they have been placed in the earth, and dissolved in it, will in their own time rise up, when the Word of God gives them resurrection, to the glory of God the Father. He will secure immortality for what is mortal, and will bountifully bestow incorruptibility on what is corruptible, for the power of God is made perfect in weakness. All this will come about so that we might never be puffed up to think that we have life of our own accord, or, with ungrateful minds, exalt ourselves against God, but so that we will know by experience that it is from his excellence and not from our own nature that we will endure everlastingly, and that we should never mistake the true glory of God, nor be ignorant of our own nature, but should know what God is able to achieve and what benefits humankind can receive from him, and that we should never be baulked of the true understanding of what God and humankind are really like. (AH V.2.3)

What Irenaeus tells us of his understanding of the Eucharist is, of course, largely conditioned by his polemical programme. 'Our teaching', he says, 'is in accord with the Eucharist and the Eucharist, in its turn, confirms our teaching' (AH IV.18.5). Nevertheless, in his relatively sparse remarks on the subject, he does reveal one or two aspects of his doctrine of the Eucharist which seem not related to the polemical purpose at hand. He is insistent, for example, that Eucharistic offerings are not made because God needs them, requires them or profits from them. God has no need of our oblations; but he allows us to make them because we have a need to make them: they give us the opportunity to be fruitful and grateful. Our offerings do not give glory to God, but, properly offered, they bring glory on us.[21] But mere external ritual will not appease God, or purify the one who performs it. Oblation and sacrifice do not confer holiness upon the person who makes them but rather are made holy by the pure conscience of the one who offers them. Sacrifice may seem to be offered properly and legitimately and in purity, but if in reality it is made without inner charity and justice towards one's neighbour and fear of God it will be of no avail (AH IV.18.3). Both these points may reflect an anxiety within Irenaeus' church, or his source, to distinguish Christian from pagan worship. The need to make such a distinction may partly have been due to the development of hieratic, ritualized forms of liturgical prayer within the church of the second century, in place of the more charismatic, unstructured liturgies indicated by the *Didache* and Justin Martyr's *Apology*.

SCRIPTURE, TRADITION AND CHURCH ORDER

Irenaeus never identifies the Church with its hierarchy. The Church is the whole body of Christ, all those who are adopted as sons of God and therefore constitute the assembly of the gods. There is only one God and one economy for the salvation of his earth creature. All humanity has its first head in Adam and its second in Christ. This ontological unity of the Church is expressed in the identity of its beliefs about God and his saving purpose, and it was the polemical utility of the concept of doctrinal unity that made Irenaeus one of the earliest theologians to celebrate the unity of the universal Church. If orthodox Christians in all the lands surrounding the Mediterranean, and even in the barbarous regions beyond, can be shown to hold the same basic doctrines, then, he argues, those doctrines must be the original and authentic ones, and doctrines held only by the gnostics, Marcion, or other heretics must be deviant.[22] The unity Irenaeus celebrates is ontological and doctrinal, not organizational or bureaucratic. Christians are limbs of the one body of which Christ is the head. In their union in Christ the one God will fulfil his one economy of salvation for the creature fashioned from the earth. The observable unity of Christians arises not from uniformity of government or ritual, but from their common belief in the one God and in his single saving purpose. Nevertheless, the emergence of hierarchical structures is discernible in Irenaeus' work, and related directly to the defence of doctrinal unity.

Ever since Paul had sought to defend the authenticity of his teaching by claiming that it was a 'handing over' of what he had himself been taught by the Lord,[23] 'tradition' has played a key role in the defence and elaboration of Christian doctrine. Clement of Rome appealed to tradition in defence of his claim that the church ministers whom he calls 'bishops and deacons' were appointed by divine authority.[24] Nothing was more natural than that, when Irenaeus undertook the unmasking and overturning of false gnosis, he should suppose the appeal to tradition to be one of his most effective weapons. Unfortunately, he had been pre-empted by the gnostics themselves, who had turned the appeal to tradition to their own purposes. In order to see how Irenaeus wrested the argument back from them, and the prominence his strategy gave to the ecclesiastical hierarchy, we need to look a little more closely at the theological methods of those he opposed.

Many of the gnostic sects classed Christians in two groups, each of which had its distinctive access to divine revelation and its distinctive religious response. The religious response of the gnostics themselves, the truly spiritual ones, was knowledge. Lesser Christians had to make do with faith and works (AH I.6.1–2). These ordinary Christians had relatively straightforward Scriptures:

bloodcurdling stories and moral tales about their just, jealous and vengeful God, which would encourage them in the life of faith and good works upon which their modified salvation would depend (AH II.29.1). The gnostics, on the other hand, were above faith and good works, just as their God was above the God of ordinary Christians. The knowledge that saved them was revealed to them either by means of an esoteric interpretation of those Scriptures which were also available to ordinary Christians, or by means of secret Scriptures, kept hidden from ordinary Christians.[25] But, for ordinary and gnostic Christians alike, Christ was the revealer, and therefore the authenticity of the doctrines of both groups had to be established by appeal to a tradition going back to Christ. For both groups, this tradition was normally guaranteed by reference to the Apostles. Hence, many of the gnostic texts which have survived, like the books of the New Testament, claim authorship by one or another of the disciples of Jesus. The gnostic Ptolemy told Flora that, if God permitted, she would learn more in the future, when she was 'counted worthy of the apostolic tradition which we also have received by succession, because we can prove all our statements from the teaching of the Saviour'.[26]

So long as both sides insisted that theirs was the authentic tradition, no progress could be made. How was one to differentiate between two contradictory sets of beliefs both claiming to have been handed on from the same set of Apostles? If Irenaeus was to meet the challenge of the gnostics he would need to establish a claim that he held the authentic Scriptures and the authentic tradition and that his opponents did not. He achieved this by calling into play the succession lists of the leaders of various churches of supposedly apostolic foundation and showing that the apostolic tradition of these churches predated the novelties of the heretics. Hegesippus had drawn up such a list for Rome, and possibly for other ancient churches, and his purpose may have been very much the same as Irenaeus'.[27] As Irenaeus puts the case, if Christ handed on any secret teaching to the Apostles, then that teaching would have been preserved in the churches founded by the Apostles, for they would surely have handed on anything they had received from the Lord, secret or otherwise, to those whom they had appointed to be leaders of the churches in their place. But we do not find the secret tradition of the gnostics in those churches, and therefore, these so-called traditions are simply inventions of recent date, while the doctrines actually found in churches of apostolic foundation are the doctrines passed on, in all their fullness, to those churches by the Apostles, and thus from Christ (AH III.3.1-2; V.20.1-2).

It is fundamental to the logic of Irenaeus' argument that tradition cannot change, or grow, or develop. It is not, in this sense, alive. Since the faith is everywhere one and the same it is equally immune from improvement in the discourse of an eloquent leader of the Church as it is from diminution in the mumbling of an inarticulate one (AH I.10.2). Bishops and teachers of the Church are not there to develop the tradition, they are there simply to hand it on. W. Wigan Harvey, whose edition of *Adversus Haereses* was published twelve years after the *Essay on the Development of Christian Doctrine*, refers pointedly, although anonymously, to John Henry Newman's book in a note to the text of Irenaeus which I have just paraphrased. 'At least here', he says, 'there is no reserve made in favour of any theory of development. If ever we find any trace of this dangerous delusion in Christian antiquity, it is uniformly the plea of heresy.'[28] He quotes Tertullian in support: 'The Valentinians allow themselves the same licence as Valentinus, the Marcionites as Marcion: to invent belief at their own whim'.[29] Harvey accurately reflects Irenaeus' position. A tradition with the potential to develop would ideally suit the gnostic cause, and be utterly fatal for Irenaeus'.

Tradition, for Irenaeus, does not mean a body of doctrine distinct from the Scriptures. Scripture and tradition are, indeed, distinct, but they are not parallel sources of doctrine. It was the heretics who claimed that their tradition gave them access to teachings not contained in the Scriptures (AH III.2.1). Irenaeus appeals to tradition not because Scripture is inadequate, but because, as the very existence of heresy shows, it is open to misinterpretation.[30] The function of tradition is to guarantee that the orthodox interpretation of the Scriptures is the correct one: that the way the Church interprets the recorded words of Jesus is the way the Apostles interpreted them when they were written down. Tradition shows the heretical interpretation to be wrong because it is novel: it was not known in apostolic churches before the arrival of the heretics (AH III.3.1-3).

In one sense, Scripture itself is part of tradition: the Apostles first proclaimed the Gospel by word, and only afterwards 'by the will of God, handed it on to us in the Scriptures' (AH III.1.1). Although the Scriptures are perfect, 'inasmuch as they are spoken by the Word of God and by his Spirit' (AH II.28.2), because the content of Scripture and tradition is identical, Irenaeus is able to say that Scripture is not necessary:

119

What if the Apostles had not left us the Scriptures? Would we not then have followed the order of the tradition which they handed on to those to whom they entrusted the churches? There are many Christians amongst the barbarians, who have salvation written not in ink on paper but in their hearts by the Spirit, and they carefully guard the ancient tradition . . . Those who have believed this faith without the aid of writing are barbarians so far as our language is concerned, but so far as concerns their minds and their customs and their manner of life they are, through their faith, most wise, and they are pleasing to God, living in all justice and chastity and wisdom. Should anyone declare to them in their own language the fictions of the heretics they would immediately stop their ears and flee far away lest they be obliged to listen to such blasphemous talk. (AH III.4.2)

The heretics are very clever in their manipulation and distortion of the Scriptures, but they will not mislead anyone, Irenaeus says, who holds fast to 'the unchanging rule of truth, which was received in baptism' (AH I.9.4). Irenaeus several times refers to this rule of truth, and its connection with baptism suggests a credal formula. However, it does not appear to have had a fixed form, but to have been adaptable to the polemical context in which it was invoked. Its fundamental features are that there is but one God, who created everything from nothing by his Word, and who is the Father of Jesus and the author of the whole history of salvation.[31]

It is surely no accident that the rule of truth, as it appears in the pages of Irenaeus, contradicts the heretics on the points on which he is most in conflict with them. No doubt, had the views he opposed been different, this would have been reflected in his presentation of the content of the rule of truth. But Irenaeus does not and cannot grant that the Church or the bishops or the teachers of the Church, as bearers of the tradition, can determine what the content of the tradition is. If a place in the apostolic succession confers authority to determine, discover or develop the tradition, then one need only claim such a place in order to be able to claim apostolic authority for whatever one teaches, which is just what the gnostics did. It is only because the successors of the Apostles are presumed to have been faithful in their duty of handing on the apostolic tradition unchanged that Irenaeus can appeal to them to show that the 'developed' doctrines of the gnostics were, in fact, alien to the authentic teaching of the Apostles. Irenaeus does allow that when disputes arise on trifling matters one ought to have recourse to the most ancient churches, in which the Apostles were active, and to find there a solution to the present problem (AH III.4.1). However, one apostolic church cannot be judged by the tradition of another because the tradition will be held equally in all apostolic churches and in all churches which concur with them (AH III.3.2). This is why Irenaeus cannot admit the possibility of a disagreement arising between apostolic churches on matters of importance, matters bearing upon the rule of truth. When the apostolic churches of Asia fell out with other Eastern apostolic churches, and with the apostolic church of Rome, on the question of the proper day for the celebration of Easter, Irenaeus vigorously objected to Rome's attempt to force the Quartodecimans into submission by threats of excommunication, even though he personally agreed with the Roman practice regarding the date of Easter. He invoked the memory of Polycarp of Smyrna and of Anicetus of Rome. Despite heated disagreement on this very issue, and strenuous and unsuccessful attempts to convince one another to change, they remained at peace, and the Bishop of Smyrna accepted the invitation of the Bishop of Rome to preside at the Eucharist they celebrated together.[32]

One famous passage of *Adversus Haereses* is still sometimes quoted as though it were an early witness to the authority of the church of Rome over other churches. The Latin translation of AH III.3.2 could be taken to mean that, because of the pre-eminent authority of the church of Rome, every other church should be in agreement with it. It is now generally agreed that Irenaeus was badly served by his translator, and that he spoke not of the pre-eminent authority of the church of Rome but of its more excellent origin. It was distinguished from other churches of apostolic foundation by the fact that it was founded by two Apostles, and by Peter and Paul, the most glorious of them, at that. It was for this reason that Irenaeus chose to give the succession list of the Roman church. The doctrines taught in other churches of apostolic foundation will automatically be in agreement with that of the church of Rome and, therefore, he may absolve himself of the tedious task of reciting their succession lists.[33]

Irenaeus' use of the Roman succession list, and his habit of referring to Roman bishops by their numbered place in it, could be taken to suggest that he regarded it as normal for a church to be presided over by only one bishop.[34] However, he offers no other evidence in support of this, and there are hints in his writings that he was familiar with the more collegial form of church government evident in the New Testament and other early Christian sources, such as the *Didache*, the first *Letter* of Clement, and the *Shepherd of Hermas*. Although at one place he appears to distinguish between bishops and presbyters (AH III.14.2), he also refers to the leaders of the churches, those to whom the Apostles entrusted the tradition, as presbyters.[35] Nowhere does it clearly appear that he used 'presbyter' of an individual entrusted with the sole government of a local church. However, if a system of government by only one bishop was not fully fledged in all of the churches with which Irenaeus was familiar, its introduction was not long to be delayed, and, indeed, the logic of the argument for apostolic succession required it. For a group or college of overseers or elders was just as likely to be divided in its opinion in the second century as in the twentieth. The concentration of ultimate authority in the hands of one individual ought to guarantee a firm, univocal resolution to a disputed question in a way that government by a college of elders could not.[36]

THE KINGDOM

One of the most surprising things about the rapid early growth of Christianity is that it was achieved in the face of the evident non-fulfilment of one of its most startling and most fundamental claims. Jesus and his earliest disciples believed that the Reign of God was to be established on the earth in the very near future. It did not happen. Still it has not happened, and yet belief in the Kingdom of God continues to sustain the religious attitude of millions of Christians. The New Testament itself shows ample evidence of various attempts to explain, or explain away, the curious non-eventfulness of the Kingdom of God. One explanation, which recommends itself to many Christians today, is to say that the Kingdom of God has happened, and those who cannot recognize it are looking in the wrong place. It is a mistake, they say, to suppose that the Kingdom was to be a this-worldly, socio-political reality. On the contrary, the Kingdom of God is a purely spiritual reality, and exists within the minds and hearts of believers. Thus, in the Authorized Version of Luke's Gospel, we find Jesus saying to the Pharisees: 'The kingdom of God cometh not with observation: Neither shall they say, Lo here! or, lo there! for, behold, the kingdom of God is within you' (Luke 17: 20–21). Even the most contemporary defenders of this purely spiritual, individualistic understanding of the Kingdom must quote from the Authorized Version, because more modern English translations do not allow the final phrase to justify it.[37] The RSV gives 'the Kingdom of God is in the midst of you'; the Jerusalem Bible and the New English Bible give 'the kingdom of God is among you'.

Irenaeus belonged to a body of Christians, surprisingly large even at the end of the second century, who continued to believe in the imminent coming of the Kingdom of God in a quite literal sense: they believed that at the coming of Christ the earth would be renewed and the just would rise from the dead to dwell with him in his Kingdom for a thousand years. The Latin and Greek words for 'thousand' have led to this view being described as millenarianism or chiliasm. Half a century later, partly in consequence of the growing influence of Platonism within Christian theology, the 'spiritual' interpretation of the coming of the Kingdom had triumphed, and the views of Irenaeus and other like-minded theologians on the Kingdom were derived as naïve or outlandish. Dionysius, Bishop of Alexandria about the middle of the third century, wrote treatises against the literal understanding of the Kingdom, especially as set forth in the Book of Revelation.[38] A century and a half later, Jerome would suppose, incorrectly, that Dionysius had written these works specifically against Irenaeus.[39] Eusebius of Caesarea traced the literal belief 'that there will be a certain period of a thousand years, after the resurrection from the dead, when the kingdom of Christ will be established in a bodily way on this earth' to Papias, who showed himself by his writings to be a man of 'exceedingly slight intelligence', and who 'came to these views through a misunderstanding of the apostolic narratives'.[40] When expounding his own views on the matter, Irenaeus had referred approvingly to Papias' writings, describing him as one who had heard John and been a comrade of Polycarp (AH V.33.4). Eusebius believed that Papias had no claim to have been a 'disciple and eye-witness of the holy Apostles',[41] but that very many churchmen, including Irenaeus, impressed by his closeness to the times of the Apostles, had been misled into accepting his views about the earthly Kingdom.[42]

Irenaeus was aware that his theology of the last times was already under censure by other orthodox churchmen, and was not afraid to counter-attack in the pages of *Adversus Haereses*, although he refrains from naming these ecclesiastical adversaries.[43] For these theologians, in the starkest contrast to Irenaeus, what really mattered was the spiritual dimension in the human being: the spirit or the soul. As with the gnostics, the goal of humankind was to ascend to the realm of pure being, to God himself. But, as God is spiritual, it is only the spiritual dimension that can be concerned in this salvation. Irenaeus, and those who continued his struggle against the gnostics, succeeded at least in preventing these Platonizing theologians from describing the body, and material creation in general, as evil, or from denying it any role in the economy of salvation. Nevertheless, for the most part, these theologians were embarrassed by the body, and were inclined to say, as Origen later did, that it was joined to the soul as a punishment because of some previous rebellion against God.[44] The life to come, in this scheme of things, will be a place or state of spiritual union between the soul and God. References in the Scriptures to the resurrection of the body had to be allegorized, or understood in a spiritual sense. The body might indeed be raised from the dead, but it would be, as even St Paul had said (1 Cor 15: 42–44), a spiritual body.

So much of Irenaeus' own fight had been in favour of the positive value of the material creation, and especially of the human body, that he could not countenance so spiritualizing an interpretation. Moreover, although no foe of allegorical exegesis when it suited him, he argued that to interpret the Scriptures which spoke of a real resurrection of the dead in a spiritual, allegorical manner was to misinterpret them (AH V.35.1–2).

Obviously, if God had planned so great an economy for the sake of a body formed from mud, that body could not lose its significance when the economy reached its goal. The kingdom promised by Jesus was to be not simply a spiritual union of souls with God but an earthly kingdom, a place where the promises made to Abraham and the patriarchs would at last be fulfilled (AH V.30.4; 32.1–2).

The fact that Irenaeus' views on the Kingdom were so soon overtaken within the Great Church by the Platonizing, spiritualizing interpretation may have a good deal to do with the general neglect of his writings in the later tradition of the Church. Most mediaeval manuscripts of *Adversus Haereses* do not contain the final chapters of Book V, where Irenaeus' eschatology is most fully presented. The desire to protect Irenaeus' reputation for orthodoxy has not been confined to mediaeval copyists. In 1938 V. Cremers attempted to show that these pages were not the work of Irenaeus at all, but a later interpolation.[45] Some scholars, though not embarrassed by the realism of Irenaeus' expectations of the Kingdom, have yet been at pains to urge that 'there is not a single mention of the words "thousand years" throughout Irenaeus' description of the Kingdom of the Son'; that he has studiously avoided 'the doctrine of the "thousand years' reign"', so that it cannot be said that there are any 'misplaced chiliastic tendencies in the *Adversus Haereses*'.[46] However, the Armenian version of *Adversus Haereses* IV and V, first published in 1910, shows these claims to be unsupportable. For from it we learn that even the one Latin manuscript which had been thought to preserve the whole of the text did, in fact, lack a small but crucial paragraph in the very heart of Irenaeus' discussion of this subject. And in that paragraph Irenaeus speaks unequivocally of the thousand-year reign of the just:[47]

> therefore John clearly foresaw the first resurrection of the just and the inheritance of the earth in the kingdom, and the prophets too had prophesied concerning it in the same terms (cf. Rev 20:4-6). This is also what the Lord taught, when he promised that he would drink a new mingling of the cup with his disciples in the kingdom. *And he promised it again when he said 'the days are coming when the dead in their tombs will hear the voice of the Son of Man and those who have done good will rise to the resurrection of life but those who have done evil will rise to the resurrection of judgement' (cf. John 5:28-29). Here he says that those who do good will rise first and go to their rest and then those who are to be judged will rise, just as the Book of Genesis says that the completion of this world is on the sixth day, that is, in the six thousandth year, and then will come the seventh day, the day of rest, of which David says, 'this is my rest, the just shall enter it' (cf. Pss 132:14 and 118:20). This is the seventh thousand years of the kingdom of the just, in which the just shall grow accustomed to incorruptibility, when the whole of creation will be renewed for those who have been preserved for this.*[48]

There is now a considerable consensus to the effect that, whatever sources he might have drawn on, the theology of the last times set forth towards the end of *Adversus Haereses* is integral to Irenaeus' theological vision.[49] It is a curious paradox that, having for so long been thought problematic, these last chapters of the work should now be among those that most recommend Irenaeus to the contemporary reader.

Much of Irenaeus' eschatology is based upon prophetic and apocalyptic literature, from both the Old and the New Testaments, and particularly upon the Book of Revelation. These works, Irenaeus insisted, must be interpreted literally, not allegorically, though he does himself sometimes interpret them in ways that we could not regard as literal (AH V.35.1–2). Irenaeus' quarrel, however, was not about the rightness or wrongness of the allegorical interpretation of Scripture generally. What was at issue here was his deeply held belief that Christians are to look forward to a this-worldly kingdom of the just. His rejection of the new 'spiritualizing' of eschatological belief was dictated by the whole of his theological outlook. The human being is made up of body, soul, and Spirit. The Spirit of humankind needs no salvation, for it is divine. What does need salvation, and what the Scriptures suggest the whole economy of salvation is centred upon, is the body, fashioned from mud by the hands of God to be in his own image and likeness. The goal of the economy is incorruptibility, and incorruptibility is not, in the strict sense, a property that can be attributed to Spirit or soul. Spirit and soul are, by nature, incapable of disintegrating, because they are not composite in the first place. So the promise of incorruptibility and immortality is hollow if it is a promise about the future of the soul or Spirit. The real miracle of the economy of salvation is that incorruptibility and immortality are to be bestowed on precisely that element which is by nature corruptible and mortal, namely, the body.

Precisely because human beings have bodies, and will only be human beings so long as they do have bodies, it is absurd for them to aspire to any kind of monistic union with God as Spirit. Bodies, even glorified bodies, impose certain limitations on the Spirit conjoined to them. They need earth to walk on, food to eat, and space to move in. Nor will they be able to avoid the bodies of other human beings walking on the earth and moving about in its space. Human society is a direct and inescapable consequence of our being embodied. So long as we are embodied, we will never be able to avoid it or do without it. So the kingdom of the just will be a social and political reality, not just a physical one. Abraham left his own people and became a pilgrim with the Word, so that he might become a fellow citizen (*politeuthē*) with the Word (AH IV.5.3). It was *land* that God promised to the descendants of Abraham, and that promise will not be fulfilled until the children of Abraham dwell in a land where they will drink the new wine promised to his disciples by Jesus (AH V.33.1–3). This kingdom, which Irenaeus calls the Kingdom of the Son, will be of lengthy but finite duration. Irenaeus proposes that each of the days of creation lasts a thousand years, by which he may have meant simply a very long time.[50] Humankind was created on the sixth day, and the course of human history occupies the sixth of the thousand-year periods of creation. The seventh thousand-year period will be occupied by the Kingdom of the Son.

Before the coming of Christ, the Antichrist will establish a kingdom in the earthly Jerusalem and reign there for a period of three years and six months, taking his seat in the Temple of God.[51] Jerusalem is said to be the seat of the Antichrist because Irenaeus identifies him with the abomination of desolation of Matthew 24:15. But Irenaeus does not pass up the opportunity to refer yet again to the failure of the Jews to accept Jesus as the Christ. Amazingly, in a context in which we have been warned off allegorical interpretation of Scripture, Irenaeus further identifies the Antichrist with the unjust judge of Luke 18:2. The widow who in the parable was ultimately able to obtain justice from him through her persistence has become for Irenaeus a symbol of Jerusalem, 'the widow who has forgotten God' (AH V.25.4). The reign of the Antichrist will be a time of much tribulation for the Church (AH V.26.1). He will recapitulate in himself the apostasy of Satan, and all the evil and deceit which that has brought about in the history of humankind.[52] In the end, Christ himself will come and cast him into the burning lake (AH V.28.2; 30.4). Then the just will rise from the dead and dwell in a renewed earthly Jerusalem. They will not die, rather they will learn to forget to die and grow accustomed to immortality, and to the vision of the Father.[53] At the end of the Kingdom of the Son, the wicked will rise to be judged and cast into the lake of fire (cf. Rev 20:13–15) (AH V.35.2). The Son, having destroyed his last enemy, which is death (cf. 1 Cor 15:24–28), will surrender his Kingdom to the Father, God will be all in all, and the everlasting reign of the Father will begin. There will be a new heaven and a new earth, and the heavenly Jerusalem will descend to the new earth (AH V.35.2; 36.1). Those judged worthy will enter heaven, others will enjoy the delights of the garden of Paradise, others will possess the beauty of the City, but all will see God, according to their capacity, and all will go on increasing in their capacity to know and love him (AH V.36.1–2). What the Father's Kingdom, the Kingdom of Heaven, will hold for us we cannot say, for Scripture tells us nothing on the point except that 'no eye has seen, nor ear heard, nor the heart of man conceived, what God has prepared for those who love him' (1 Cor 2:9) (AH V.36.3).

Unlike some other early Christian theologians, Irenaeus has very little interest in the punishment of the wicked. The fires of hell, he says, were intended by God not for humankind, but for Satan, the chief of apostasy, and the other rebellious angels.[54] Human beings will end up there only if they are seduced into apostasy with them (AH V.26.2). Nor does the Judgement reveal a vindictive God condemning to punishment those who displease him (AH V.27.2). The meaning of the word judgement is separation (AH V.27.1). God created all alike with the ability to make free choices: by their free choices human beings separate themselves into the just and the unjust. The just remain in the obedient love of God and are the recipients of his bounty. The unjust separate themselves from God, and the divine judgement is simply a recognition of this self-willed separation, which entails death, and the loss of all God's bounty (AH V.27.2). Irenaeus suggests that hell is not so much a place of physical torment, as a self-imposed condition of misery: the misery of those who, although surrounded by brilliant light, stumble about in darkness, not because they cannot see, but because they will not: it is not the light that blinds them, rather they blind themselves to the light.[55] Like Adam in the garden, they hide from the sight of God, even though they have nowhere to hide except among his creatures.[56] They refuse to open their eyes to the only reality there is—one God who created one universe for one purpose only, to bring his earth creature fully to life, made incorruptible by union with his own Spirit, resplendent with that glory of the Father which is visible in the humanity of his Son.

Notes

1 AH IV.25.1; cf. III.5.3.

2 Cf. Matt 3:9, Luke 3:8 and AH IV.7.2; 8.1; 25.1; V.32.2; 34.1; Dem 93-94.

3 AH III.21.1; IV.33.4; V.1.3.

4 AH IV.20.12; cf. Exod 2:21.

5 AH IV.20.12; cf. Joshua 2:1-21.

6 Jerome, *Commentariorum in Mattheum Libri IV* (Corpus Christianorum LXXVII; 1969), p. 195; B. M. Metzger, *A Textual Commentary on the Greek New Testament* (London: United Bible Societies, 1971).

7 AH IV.21.2-3; cf. Rom 9:10-13 and Gen 25:23-26.

8 AH IV.21.3; cf. Gen 29 - 30.

9 Cf. 'The Martyrs of Lyons' in Herbert Musurillo (ed.), *The Acts of the Christian Martyrs* (Oxford, 1972), pp. 76, 84 (= Eusebius, *Church History* V.1.45-46; 2.6).

10 AH IV.8.1; cf. Luke 13:28–29, Matt 8:11–12.

11 There is a small amount of quite ancient evidence that the *Magnificat* was originally attributed to Elizabeth. At AH III.10.2 Irenaeus attributes it to Mary, but this is quite possibly a scribal correction, just as some manuscripts attribute it to Mary at AH IV.7.1.

12 AH III.16.6; 19.3; IV.25.3; 37.7; V.18.2.

13 AH III.19.1; IV.25.3; 31.2.

14 AH III.6.1; cf. Ps 82:1.

15 AH I.21.1; III.17.3; IV.14.2; V.18.2.

16 AH III.12.7; 20.2; IV.22.1; 31.2; V.14.2–3; 15.3.

17 AH III.17.1; cf. 9.3; V.20.2.

18 AH III.24.1; IV.33.9–10; Dem 94.

19 AH IV.17.5; 18.4; V.2.2–3.

20 AH V.2.3; cf. 2.2.

21 AH IV.17.5; 18.1, 3, 6.

22 AH I.10.2; cf. III.4.3.

23 1 Cor 11:23; cf. 11:2; 15:3; 2 Thess 2:15; 3:6.

24 Clement, *Letter to the Corinthians* 42.

25 AH I.20.1; 25.5; III.2.1; 11.9.

26 Epiphanius, *Panarion* 33.9 in W. Foerster, *Gnosis: A Selection of Gnostic Texts*, Eng. translation ed. R. McL. Wilson, I (Oxford, 1971), p. 161.

27 Eusebius, *Church History* IV.22.3.

28 W. W. Harvey (ed.), *Sancti Irenaei Libros quinque Adversus Haereses* I (Cambridge, 1857), p. 94.

29 Tertullian, *De Praescriptione Haereticorum* 42.8.

30 AH I.1.3; 3.6; 8.1; 9.1, 3; II.praef.1; 10.1; 27.3; III.12.12; 21.3; IV.26.1; V.13.5.

31 AH I.22.1; II.28.1; III.11.1; IV.35.4; cf. Dem 3.

32 Eusebius, *Church History* V.24.11–18. Quartodecimans were Christians who celebrated Easter on the same day as the Jewish Passover, the fourteenth day of the month Nisan, and not on the following Sunday.

33 The best of the multitudinous studies of this passage is L. Abramowski, 'Irenaeus Adv. Haer. III.3.2: Ecclesia Romana and omnis ecclesia and *ibid.* 3.3. Anacletus of Rome', *Journal of Theological Studies* 28 (1977), pp. 101–4.

34 AH I.27.1; III.3.3; 4.3.

35 AH IV.26.2, 4, 5; 32.1; V.5.1; 36.2.

36 Of course, government by a single bishop only works as a means of ensuring uniformity of teaching so long as all members of a church regard the same person as the lawful bishop. It soon happened that sections of a community which did not agree with the bishop regarded him as no bishop and set up another as the authentic guarantor of apostolic faith. At one point in the fourth century there were three claimants to the apostolic see of Antioch. Today there are at least five.

37 A. N. Wilson, in *Jesus* (London, 1992), seems willing to admit that Jesus may have taught that his kingdom would come in human history (p. 217; cf. pp. 140-1), but nevertheless favours the Tolstoyan view that 'the Kingdom is within us, and not of this world; that the true followers of Jesus can therefore never wish to take part in civil systems, and never seek political solutions to the problems which beset society' (p. 252; cf. pp. 115, 163).

38 Eusebius, *Church History* VII.24-25.

39 Jerome, *In Esaiam* XVIII prol.

40 *Church History* III.39.12-13.

41 *Church History* III.39.2.

42 *Church History* III.39.13.

43 AH V.31.1; cf. A. Orbe, 'Adversarios anónimos de la Salus Carnis', *Gregorianum* 60 (1979), pp. 9-53; *Teología de San Ireneo: Comentario al Libro V del 'Adversus haereses'* I (Madrid, 1987), pp. 129ff.

44 Origen, *De Principiis* I.4.1; 7.4; 8.1, 4; II.8.3.

45 V. Cremers, 'Het millenarisme van Irenaeus', *Bijdragen der Nederlandsche Jesuieten* I (1938), pp. 28-80.

46 G. Wingren, *Man and the Incarnation*, trans, R. Mackenzie (Edinburgh and London, 1959), pp. 189-90, and other authors cited there.

47 Remarkably enough, A. Orbe, who has no quarrel with the 'Irenaean' quality of this paragraph, has suggested that it may have been added by someone well acquainted with Irenaeus' thought, or even by Irenaeus himself in a later edition, on the ground that there is a more harmonious and logical flow without the 'addition': *Teología de San Ireneo* III, pp. 617-18.

48 AH V.36.3. The asterisks mark the section known only from the Armenian.

49 See, for example, R. Tremblay, *La manifestation et la vision de Dieu selon saint Irénée de Lyon* (Münster, 1978), p. 88, note 81.

50 AH V.28.3. Cf. 2 Pet 3:8: 'with the Lord one day is as a thousand years, and a thousand years as one day'.

51 AH V.25.1, 3-4; 30.4. In his 1702 edition of *Adversus Haereses* Grabe proposed that the derivation of three-and-a-half years from the 'half

130

of the week' (i.e. three-and-a-half days) mentioned in Daniel 9:27 had already been made in Revelation 12:6 and 12:14.

52 AH V.25.1, 5; 28.2; 29.2; 30.1.

53 AH V.32.1; 35.1–2; 36.2–3.

54 AH III.23.3; cf. V.27.1.

55 AH V.13.2; 27.2; cf. III.20.1; IV.29.1–2; 39.3–4.

56 Cf. AH V.15.4.

8

An outstanding Christian thinker?

Hitherto, although I have not attempted to conceal my own admiration for and sympathy with the theology of Irenaeus, I have not been particularly at pains to show why he deserves to be included in a series devoted to outstanding Christian thinkers.

On some reckonings of what counts as being an outstanding thinker, Irenaeus would score poorly. This is especially so if groundbreaking originality of mind and a profound and enduring influence on the thought of those who follow are judged to be hallmarks of an outstanding thinker. Irenaeus would have been deeply offended had it been suggested to him that he was an original thinker. The original thinkers of his time were the gnostics, Marcion and other heretics. Their originality of thought was, in Irenaeus' view, precisely what was wrong with them, and it was their novel views he attacked, in defence of what he supposed to be the traditional teaching of the Church, handed down unchanged and unchanging. Leaving to one side the matter of direct and unacknowledged quotation of other writers, Irenaeus is unlikely to have been embarrassed by the accusation that he derived all his theological insights from others. For what he claimed to be defending and proclaiming was, so he said, identical with what every other orthodox preacher defended and proclaimed:

> having received this kerygma and this faith, the Church, although scattered throughout the world, diligently keeps it, as though inhabiting a single dwelling; it believes these things in the same way, as though it had but one heart and one soul, and it preaches

and teaches and hands them on in the same way, as though it had but one mouth. For although the languages of the world differ, yet the force of the tradition is one and the same. Nor do the churches founded in Germany believe differently or hand on differently; nor do those amongst the Iberians, or those amongst the Celts, nor do those in the Orient, or those in Egypt or those in Libya, or those settled on the Mediterranean seaboard; but just as the sun, the creature of God, is one and the same through the world, so the light, the preaching of the truth, shines everywhere and enlightens all those who wish to come to the knowledge of the truth. (AH I.10.2)

From our point of view, this confidence may be considered naïve. For the 'early catholicism' which Irenaeus represents was a relatively new phenomenon, even in his time; as a coherent and functioning system, it is hardly traceable earlier than the first decades of the second century. There is wide scope for argument that Irenaeus' view of the uniformity of unchanging tradition was rosier than the facts allowed. We have noted, for example, that he was in conflict with other theologians within the Great Church on the question of the resurrection of the dead and the Kingdom. To what extent Irenaeus is a faithful reporter of the chief religious beliefs of the emerging mainstream Christian Church, to what extent he has imposed his own synthesis on those beliefs, we cannot truly say, for too little of the writings of his contemporaries has survived. We do, however, have his own word that he is recording the unchanging faith of the universal church, and we may surmise that his writings met with initial popularity.[1] We know that later, even if he was largely unread, his orthodoxy went generally unchallenged.

It may be that history was kind to Irenaeus in forgetting him for so long. Other theologians were less fortunate. For centuries after his death, Origen's writings would be brought into court and condemned for their divergence from the then prevailing standards of orthodoxy. For, although Irenaeus would abhor the thought, the tradition does change, and theologians who do not change with it can find themselves indignantly repudiating the accusation of heresy for views which they had been brought up in the Catholic Church to consider thoroughly orthodox. It was so with Arius, with Nestorius, with Pelagius, and with many others. In modern times Irenaeus has been appealed to as a witness to the Catholic teaching on tradition, but, in truth, his teaching is radically different from the latter. Even while quoting Irenaeus, the Dogmatic Constitution on Divine Revelation of the Second Vatican Council speaks of tradition in a way which would have deeply perplexed him:

> This tradition which comes from the Apostles progresses in the church under the assistance of the holy Spirit. There is growth in understanding of what is handed on, both the words and the realities they signify. This comes about through contemplation and study by believers . . . through the intimate understanding of spiritual things which they experience; and through the preaching of those who, on succeeding to the office of bishop, receive the sure charism of truth. Thus, as the centuries advance, the church constantly holds its course towards the fullness of God's truth, until the day when the words of God reach their fulfilment in the church.[2]

We have seen how different this is from Irenaeus' understanding of the tradition. For him, as Yves Congar noted, the 'sure charism of truth' resides not in the subject of the tradition, the church or its leadership, but in the objective tradition itself.[3] A developing, or changing, tradition clearly requires an arbiter to determine what is an authentic development and what is not. In the Constitution on Divine Revelation this function is said to be entrusted 'only to those charged with the church's ongoing teaching function'.[4] For Irenaeus, the function of leaders of churches, and especially of churches founded by the Apostles, is to witness to the unchanging tradition. They are to be obeyed not because they have authority to interpret Scripture or tradition, but because their succession from the Apostles guarantees that what is taught in their churches will be one and the same as that which is taught in every other church which possesses the unchanging tradition.

If Irenaeus is not, on his own admission, an original thinker, if, despite the enormous significance of his successful campaign against the gnostics and Marcion, he had but little positive impact on the future direction of theological speculation, should we list him among outstanding Christian thinkers? There are at least two grounds, I believe, on which we should. First there is the vastness of the enterprise he undertook. Irenaeus was not a systematic theologian, yet much of the essential subject matter of theology is covered in the works of his that have survived. This comprehensiveness was due to his desire to defeat his opponents utterly.[5] Bizarre as he no doubt found the teachings of the gnostics, Irenaeus did not waste too much time laughing at them. He accurately gauged the threat they posed to the continued existence of the form of Christianity which he regarded as normal and true, and he was determined to show, arguing from the widest possible base, that they were wrong. In consequence of this strategy he has left us a remarkably comprehensive picture of what was believed by Christians who thought themselves orthodox in the late second century.

The magnitude of the task Irenaeus undertook and brought to completion won him admiration in his own time. My second reason for suggesting that Irenaeus should be included amongst outstanding Christian thinkers has more to do with the admiration he attracts in the present. For, despite the immediately recognizable catholicism of his theology, it offers to those more used to a catholicism overshadowed by the figure of St Augustine a remarkably fresh and different outlook. Ironically, Irenaeus, the great defender of orthodoxy and unchanging tradition, allows us to see that orthodoxy is not monolithic, that before Augustine's influence exerted itself in the West there was a fully articulated orthodox theology suffused with an optimism and a confidence which have since largely disappeared from the Western tradition. It may be purely accidental that it was Irenaeus who left us a record of this other strain of orthodoxy. Had the writings of those from whom he borrowed survived instead of his own we might have an even fuller picture, and we might have grounds for applauding the powerful insights and advances of individuals. As it is, Irenaeus' claim to greatness is that he witnesses to this other tradition, and that he does so with so powerful a conviction, not only that he is right, but that his rightness is that of the Great Church, that he may suggest to his modern readers that it is possible to be orthodox and catholic and still range beyond the gloomy shadows cast by St Augustine.

The optimism of Irenaeus' outlook rests firmly on his conviction that God is one, and has only one purpose for the creature he formed from mud. It would be most misleading to say that Irenaeus thinks sin is insignificant. It is significant, but ultimately only for those who remain in it. Catastrophic as might be its effects on them, it has no catastrophic effect upon God's purposes for humankind. Sin alters the shape of that economy, but it does not call it into existence. As things have turned out, the economy has been realized by the shepherd coming in search of his lost sheep and carrying it home on his shoulders, but, even before Adam's sin, the economy was centred on the incarnation of the Son. Irenaeus will not speculate on the course the economy of salvation would have taken, or on the role of the second Adam, had the first Adam not sinned. Because he did sin, and fell under Satan's power, the second Adam re-engaged the fight with Satan and was victorious where the first Adam had been defeated. In the risen Jesus, humanity exists in an infinitely more glorious state than it did in the first Adam. But it was always intended that this should be so. Adam did not fall from a state of original justice. He was created as a 'little one', by a God who always intended that he should grow into the full stature of Christn.[6]

Irenaeus would insist as vigorously as Augustine that nothing can be achieved without grace. But he would have been appalled at the thought that God would offer grace to some and withhold it from others. The entire universe, and every human being within it, depends at every moment and in every dimension of its existence upon the will of God, who holds it in being above the nothingness from which he created it. The beneficent will of God is the substance, the underpinning, of everything that is. Whenever God acts outside himself he reveals his glory, his beauty, his grace. Every created thing is instinct with the glory of God, but nothing is intended to show forth his glory so much as his *chef d'oeuvre*, the humanity of his Son, which he has brought to the fullness of life, which lives immortal and incorruptible by the power of the Holy Spirit which dwells in it, which is radiant with the Father's light. This future is not held in reserve only for those whom God has predestined. It is freely offered to every creature formed from Adam's flesh, from the mud God took in his hands in the beginning. It is in every human being's power to receive this gift: not by stretching out a hand and grasping it, as the first Adam attempted to do, and as we all attempt to do whenever we sin, but simply by recognizing the difference between God and his creatures, by allowing that only God can create us in his image and likeness, and that, all-powerful though he is, he cannot do this unless we fully embrace the condition of creaturehood, unless we accept that we can never be perfect, but can be drawn ever closer to the glory of the uncreated God, unless we allow the creative grace of God to work upon us, unless we abandon all attempts to make something of ourselves, unless we learn to relax, in the obedience of faith, in the hands of our creator, so that he can create us, as he intended to do from the beginning, after the pattern of Christ.

Irenaeus' reaction to the heretics' denial of the bodiliness of the human condition puts one in mind of Dr Johnson's reaction to Bishop Berkeley's theory of knowledge. Asked to take seriously what appeared to be transparent nonsense, Irenaeus was perplexed and indignant, as one is when one suspects that one's leg is being pulled. He was an empiricist; the things human beings should enquire into, he thought, were the things that stared them in the face, the things God had actually presented them with (AH II.27.1). The gnostics were afloat on a sea (a 'depth') of incomprehension (AH IV.9.3). Irenaeus could not understand how educated, intelligent people could possibly believe what they taught. How could people who need to eat and drink every day, who know the pleasure of sexual arousal, and the pain of physical separation from those they love, who suffer in their bodies when ill or diseased, who know they are going to die, quite possibly in the same agony of body they have seen others endure — how could anyone who shares this common lot of all humanity suppose that the body is incidental to the business of being a human being? It is easy enough to see the attraction of the belief that the real and essential element of a human being is something spiritual, temporarily and distressingly associated with the body, but destined to be freed from it and to return to the purely spiritual realm which is its real home. This is attractive because it is escapist, but escapism is not a real option for an intelligent adult. When a small child tells you that he or she is invisible, or not of the present company, it is advisable to play along. To do otherwise is to invite foot-stamping and tears. When seemingly intelligent adults ask you to believe something similar, the humane thing to do is to try to bring them to their senses.

The suffering which is so much part of the human condition is not due to the misfortune of the soul or spirit's enmeshment in the body. It is due to the fact that the body has been bruised and crushed by Satan. The redemption offered by the Christian Gospel is not a matter of the release of the soul or spirit from the malignant body, but of the body being made whole and strong again in Christ, who, in Adam's own flesh, re-engaged the conflict with Satan, defeated the ancient enemy of humankind, despoiled him of all those he had taken captive, bestowed on them the victor's prize of incorruptibility, and led them back to friendship with God.

Irenaeus was so much at pains to uphold the simple truth that it is the body that matters, that, taken out of his own context, he might appear to have assigned it too much importance. Despite his initial victory over his opponents, he was unable to arrest the growing influence of Platonism upon Christianity, and many of the essential aspirations of the gnostics were soon to find welcome, and a permanent home, within the spiritual and mystical traditions of the catholic, orthodox Church. The same Church is fortunate to have in Irenaeus' writings an enthusiastic refutation of the false understandings that ensue when those of spiritual or mystical inclination succumb to the ever-present temptation to suppose that the body is of no account in the scheme of salvation.

Modern-day critics of the social and political preoccupations of the Christian Church often betray their ignorance of its history by alleging that Christianity is essentially to do with the salvation of the soul, with the spiritual dimension of the human condition. One could appeal to many witnesses in all ages to refute this. Irenaeus' inability to reach any kind of imaginative sympathy with the gnostics arises not only from his frank evaluation of the necessity of the body, but also from the equally frank and cheerful acceptance of the fact that human beings are social animals. He was at home in the civic world of late antiquity from which the gnostics longed so desperately to escape. When expressing his disgust at the moral behaviour of some of the heretics he appeals to the standards, not of the Christians, but of his fellow citizens. The heretics, he says:

> behave in ways it is not lawful to hear about, that one could not imagine, that one would not believe were it alleged of people dwelling in our own cities. (AH I.25.4)

Although his own community had undergone a horrifying persecution by the Roman state, Irenaeus could say of the Romans that 'the world is at peace because of them, and we can walk in the streets without fear and travel by sea wherever we will' (AH IV.30.3). To live in a city was natural and normal for human beings; salvation was to consist not in escape from the city, but in the perfection of social and political institutions, in a new Jerusalem, come down from heaven. From the central importance of the body in the divine economy Irenaeus draws the logical conclusion that the promised Kingdom of the Son will be a social and political reality. Modern readers will no doubt find much of the detail in Irenaeus' eschatology as quaint as did many shortly after it was written. Nevertheless, modern Christians profess belief in the resurrection of the body, and Irenaeus' teaching about the Kingdom might serve to remind them that society and politics are inescapable dimensions of being human. When Christians pray for the coming of the Kingdom they do not pray to be transferred to a supra-human condition. They pray for the fulfilment of God's purposes for humankind as he created it.

Attempts to create a theocratic society here and now have never been less than disastrous, and it would be idle and foolish to try to imagine what the social and political dimensions of the Kingdom might be like. But Christians ought to be used to living with what some philosophers call empty intentions, that is, notions with hardly any content, ideas grasped only in their shadowy, sketchy parameters. 'God', after all, is such an empty intention.[7] Irenaeus reminds us that we need to have at least such an empty intention about the Kingdom of the Son. As political and social reality is part of the human condition, we may look for these dimensions to be transformed in the Kingdom, but not taken away. Moreover, if what we are destined for is a transformation of our social and political condition, then we cannot ignore the social and political dimensions of our existence here and now. For all the folly and waywardness that may mark the involvement of Christians, as Christians, in social and political matters, they cannot be accused of meddling in what does not concern them, for such involvement is inescapable, and directly consequent upon the belief that we are all of a piece with the mud God took from the earth and is fashioning in the image and likeness of himself.

Irenaeus probably shared with many of his contemporaries and many who followed him in the early Church a primitive understanding of sexual physiology which could, and in some other authors did, lead to a gross devaluing of women in society and in the Church. But, because he thought that what matters to us most as human beings is our bodies, Irenaeus had no difficulty in assigning a place of central significance to the Virgin Mary in his understanding of the divine economy. For Irenaeus, everything depends upon the second Adam being of the same flesh as the first, taking up the conflict with Satan in that same flesh, winning the prize of immortality in and for that same flesh. Mary, whose flesh was Adam's flesh, was the guarantee of the identity between the first and second Adam. Christ was a human being because he was formed of the flesh of the human being who was his mother. Having assigned this vital physical significance to Mary, Irenaeus has no difficulty in going on to assign a significance to her moral worth, to her obedience to the Divine Word, which, rather shockingly to our ears, is paralleled to the obedience of Christ himself. By her obedience of faith she unravelled the skein of God's purpose for us, which Eve had tangled by her disobedience, just as Christ, by his obedience, reversed Adam's defeat through disobedience.

It can be difficult, and sometimes embarrassing, to disengage the Church's doctrines from the primitive understandings of the world and the body which were the unavoidable background to their formation. Nobody would suppose that any truth is to be assigned to the understanding of human conception I have outlined above (pp. 88–9). Some would argue that the doctrine of the virgin birth is so closely tied to it as to cause real theological problems for the defence of the genuine humanity of Jesus. It might, however, be heartening to observe that even so unpromising a background need not inevitably give rise to a theology in which women are devalued. It may not be an accident that Irenaeus' community at Lyons was able to say so spontaneously that one of their number, a woman, could represent Christ for them, so that 'they were able in their struggle to see, even with their outward eyes, the one who was crucified for them . . . For she had put on Christ, the great and unconquerable athlete, and had routed her adversary in many bouts and had, on account of her contest, been crowned with the crown of incorruptibility.'[8]

Notes

1   An Egyptian papyrus containing part of AH III.9.3 might date from the end of the second century (SC 210, pp. 127–8).

2   *Dei Verbum* 8: *Decrees of the Ecumenical Councils*, ed. Norman P. Tanner (London, 1990), p. 974.

3   AH IV.26.2; Yves M.-J. Congar, *Tradition and Traditions: An Historical and a Theological Essay* (London, 1966), p. 177.

4   *Dei Verbum* 10: *Decrees of the Ecumenical Councils*, p. 975.

5   AH I.31.4; II.7.1; III.2.3; IV.praef.1.

6   Dem 12; AH IV.11.1; 38.1.

7   'So long as we know God only in the ways of man, by contentious learning, by arguing and dispute, we see nothing but the shadow of Him, and in that shadow meet with many dark appearances, little certainty, and much conjecture': Jeremy Taylor (1613–67), *The Whole Works of the Right Reverend Jeremy Taylor*, ed. R. Haber and C. P. Eden (London, 1847–52), 8, p. 379. Taylor contrasted such knowledge of God with that which comes through holiness, and the 'intuition of gracious experience'. I owe this reference to the Revd Timothy Gaden.

8   'The Martyrs of Lyons' in Herbert Musurillo (ed.), *The Acts of the Christian Martyrs* (Oxford, 1972), p. 75 (=Eusebius, *Church History* V.1.41–42; my translation).

Index to Irenaeus' works